MYSTICS REVEALED

UNCONVENTIONAL SUCCESS STORIES FROM EXTRAORDINARY LEADERS

INSPIRED HEARTS PUBLISHING
NICOLETTE RASHAE HALLADAY
CHANIN ZELLNER   CHARLOTTE DE JAEGHER
CHRISTINE GLASNER   KIM TREMBLAY
KRISTEN TOSCANO   MARY GOODEN
REGYNA CURTIS   ROBIN RICHARDSON
ROXY RAPEDIUS   SHANNON OLSEN
SILKE HARVEY   SIMRAN BHATIA   TRICIA MENDES
YUMIE ZEIN

COPYRIGHT

Copyright © 2021 by Nicolette Halladay and Inspired Hearts Publishing

All rights reserved. Apart from any fair dealing for the purposes of research or private study, or criticism or review as permitted under the Copyright, Designs, and Patents Act 1988, this publication may only be reproduced, stored, or transmitted, in any form or means, with the prior permission in writing of the copyright owner, or in the case of the reprographic reproduction in accordance with the terms of licenses issued by Copyright Licensing Agency. Enquires concerning reproduction outside those terms should be sent to the publisher.

CONTENTS

1. Welcome to Mystics Revealed — 1
2. My Journey Within-Navigating the most challenging and rewarding experience of my life — 3
   Shannon Olsen — 11
3. Encounters with STRANGErs: Learning It's Safe to be Me — 13
   Regyna Curtis — 23
4. Taking a Stand for Me — 25
   Chanin Zellner — 33
5. Wisdom Between the Leaves — 35
   Charlotte De Jaegher — 45
6. Finding my Authentic Self — 47
   Kristen Toscano — 55
7. A Bath Tub — 57
   Tricia Mendes — 67
8. Keep Going — 69
   Christine Glasner — 77
9. Stepping Into The Akashic Gateway — 79
   Yumie Zein — 87
10. Surviving Blue Bird ~ A story of courage and resilience — 89
    Roxy Rapedius — 101
11. Seasons of Love, Loss and Personal Power — 103
    Kim Tremblay — 111
12. ~ So It Is — 113
    Mary Gooden — 121
13. FULFILLING LIFE-CHANGING GOALS — 123
    Robin Richardson — 131
14. Coming Home — 133
    Silke Harvey — 141
15. Simple spirituality...an act of self-love. — 143
    Simran Bhatia — 151
16. About Inspired Hearts Publishing — 153

1

WELCOME TO MYSTICS REVEALED

What is life if not felt deeply?
What is history without the stories of our people?
What is our future without the ability to self express?

Have you ever sat down to dinner with someone who poured out the details of their life to you? The major and intimate series of events that has created the person sitting in front of you?

Or maybe they share only one section in time with you.

- The moments everything changed for them
- The moments things became clear
- The moments they were unsure if they they would be be able to carry on
- When everyone in their life abandoned them or when they stood strong for themselves.
- When they lost themselves or found themselves
- Their search for belonging and self discovery

Those are the stories that pull us in. They make friends out of strangers and soulmates out of lovers. A personal invitation to see life through a new lens. Up close and personal. A glimpse at the emotions they traveled through to end up here sitting in front of you.

This book is filled with inspirational stories from the authors who have broken away from the traditional norms to achieve great success. Showing you that anything is possible if you set your mind to it and tap into your inner knowing and power. It will inspire you to find your own path and uncover the potential that is hidden inside all of us. The world needs more people like those featured in this book, who have discovered their true selves and are determined to push boundaries.

The mentors in this book have all experienced a spiritual awakening that led to a transformation in their lives. This self-discovery has enabled them to become extraordinary leaders. Each of their stories is unique, but they share common themes of courage, compassion and resilience. By connecting with these mystics, you can learn how to unleash your own potential and create a life of purpose and meaning.

If you're looking for inspiration and guidance on your own journey of self-awakening, then look no further than Mystics Revealed. These incredible individuals will show you that anything is possible when you follow your heart and embrace your true nature. So dive into their stories, connect with their wisdom, and let the magic begin!

2

MY JOURNEY WITHIN-NAVIGATING THE MOST CHALLENGING AND REWARDING EXPERIENCE OF MY LIFE

SHANNON OLSEN

Spiritual Awakening......what does that term mean and how did it completely change my life?

I would like to start out by sharing a bit about my personal experience in my own spiritual journey, some knowledge I have come across through my own research, and of course what I have learned since becoming an Angel Medium and channeling beautiful Divine messages over the past few years.

Every single one of us will begin on our own journey at the exact time we are meant to. This is definitely not something you can force, and there is usually some type of major event in our lives that begins our "awakening". This can either be a traumatic life-changing event or a positive event that nudges us to begin to shift and explore the Spirit world a little deeper.

Personally, I had always believed in the Spirit world and was obsessed at a very young age with wanting to pass healing messages to people. I always felt there was more to the world out there, there was more than I could physically touch and see, and I just had this "feeling" that I would find out more someday.

My someday came with the passing of my father. This event was the shift that pushed me into diving deeper into the spiritual world. My father had just passed away from cancer at the age of 61, and I was nine months pregnant with my first child- his first grandchild. I was riddled with feelings of how unfair this was, how could I only be 30 and already losing a parent? How is it that my dad will never hold his grandchild? As I worked through this overflowing stream of emotions and tried to make some sort of sense of it all, the Universe began to conspire and show me that there was indeed something beyond what I was seeing, something more to this story of my life that I was missing and needed to "awaken" to. This is where it all began.....

The first kind of "event" that made me think there is more, happened at my dad's funeral. I remember getting ready for the service and talking to him, asking him to help me get through this because it was the hardest thing I would ever do. It wasn't until later on the next day that I had realized the most amazing thing happened. Throughout the service, I FELT like I had support, like a peaceful "everything was ok" kind of feeling. I remember having this strength that I never experienced before as the funeral went on, and even more so as I dreaded the hardest part- following my father's casket from the service to the gravesite. The sense of love and reassurance I felt inside was like nothing I had ever experienced as I walked behind him. This string of Universal signs continued, as two people came up to me after the service separately and said "did you see that every time you went near your dad's casket the sun shone right through the window on you?"

Needless to say, I was intrigued and began researching and reading every spiritual book I could find. My personal journey was very up and down the first couple of years, and I would go through periods of diving deep into everything, and then not read or do a single spiritual thing for months. It was during this time that I learned however you are being guided is completely unique and normal for you. Trust in that and allow yourself to learn and go at your own pace. We all have only one path to follow and that is our own. The biggest lesson I have learned is to have patience with all of this and to show yourself grace. Starting to make a connection to your intuition and the spirit world is not an overnight skill you learn. It takes practice and consistency and above all patience.

I have been working on my connection and growing for 10 years now, and I still feel like I have hardly scratched the surface. I am not saying this to make it seem overwhelming, I am saying that it is a door that once you open, you will not want to close. It is so incredible, and when you begin to make tiny shifts in how you live in this world, you will never go back. It is literally like seeing everything with a new set of eyes.

My game changer in connecting to myself and my Higher Guidance came with a consistent meditation practice and the intention of finding out who I really was and what my Soul was asking me to do. This was when I began to discover my gift of connecting to the Angels, and that gift was how I was supposed to pass my healing messages, to heal myself and others in the way I had always envisioned as a child.

Everything had finally begun to click into place as I embarked on this new connection to myself and my beautiful team of Angels forever present to love, support, and guide me. I started slowly as I could manage, and once I began to be more consistent, I started noticing little shifts in my life. These shifts were mostly in the way I would react to things, and how some things that really triggered me before hardly bothered me anymore, if at all. There was almost a shift in my overall demeanor and my ability to bring myself back into a more balanced state more quickly. It is almost like you just stop worrying about a lot of the little things that used to stress you out or lower your energy. This is because when you are connected to your intuition, you are naturally in a higher state of energy, and all of those little things that are of a lower state of energy cannot help but fall away as they are no longer a match for you.

The more I continued down this path and listened to my Soul, the more shifts I began to see in my life, including being suddenly able to relinquish my need to control everything around me at all times. I cannot tell you how much stress was lifted off of my shoulders with this one small shift alone.

I became aware of this particular change around Christmas time a few years ago, as we hauled out all of our decorations for the season and my children begged me to allow them to decorate the house themselves. Now, normally this would have sent me off the deep end thinking about all of the mismatched colors, the haphazard pattern of garland strewn about, and the tree not being perfectly matched with the ornaments spaced out evenly. But for some reason that day, I simply said "Yes." I said yes before I even gave it a second thought, and was only focused on the joy I saw on their faces as they tore into the boxes and began excitedly chattering to each other as they planned their very own Christmas extravaganza. In that moment that is all that mattered, being present in their joy and making that memory.

I have found that this release of control has carried over into other areas of my life, and has benefited me in similar ways as well. By connecting to my Higher Self, and doing the inner healing my Soul was guiding me to, my perspective on a LOT of things changed. Often in ways that took me by surprise, as this experience with my children did, where my reactions came so easily and naturally that things finally felt like they just flowed.

The deeper my connection to myself became, the more inner healing I was doing, releasing of old emotions, thought patterns, limiting beliefs, the more I noticed things in my outside world shifting right along with me without any of my own efforts. This is when I knew I was on to something big, something that I knew I had to share with other women who were also craving that deep Soul connection, of coming home to themselves. I realized that the more I focused only on me and my personal healing, the more the outside stuff just fell into place.

It was absolutely mind-blowing how my own change in energy and spiritual health was changing those around me as well without even trying! This is the magic and beauty of energy and seeing first hand how positive changes in our energy bring about positive changes all around us. Here I was constantly worried and stressed about things around me that were out of my control, about the future, about all of these outside circumstances that were taking all of my energy and blinding me to the fact that the change must first come from within. Only then can the rest follow.

Consequently, I began my deepest journey yet-the path to self discovery, self-love, self-connection, and self-worth. I had no idea the impact of this journey at the time, however, now I know that it is the absolute foundation of everything. The very first brick that must be laid and built upon for us to fully live in our authentic truth connected to our Divine selves, in trust that we have all of the answers we will ever need within us and that we only must listen to hear them. Our relationship to self is one of the largest pillars that I have built my mission on, in following my passion to guide other women.

This foundation that I was slowly building has brought me many rewards and is the greatest gift that I have ever given myself. The chance to truly look deep within at who I was, and learn that for me to strengthen that relationship, I first had to accept ALL parts of myself. The light side AND the shadow side. In doing this, I was able to finally put myself and my self-care as a priority in my life because I actually KNEW I was worth it. I didn't know that before. I was ridden with guilt every time I did something for myself, I wouldn't buy new clothes because I thought that was taking away from my children having clothes, I wouldn't ever go to the spa because I thought that money could always have gone to a "better" cause, I would feel guilty for wanting to have time to myself and take a bubble bath because I thought my children would think I didn't love them if I wasn't with them constantly.

Little did I know that this guilt was merely a limiting belief pattern, a feeling of not being worthy of the love I so freely gave to others but was so reluctant to turn inward for myself. Listening to the guidance from my beautiful Angels, I dove into more inner healing to uncover where the root of these beliefs, these wounds were so that I could finally release it from my Being, and rewrite those thought patterns of guilt into patterns of self-love, self-respect, and self-worth. I began to no longer feel the guilt of taking time for myself when my Soul was asking me to, or for buying myself something that I could enjoy or that made me feel good.

Prior to this beautiful relationship to self that I have been building, any situations that came into my life that were not in my Highest interest, I would have accepted, and I would have relinquished to doing things that I did not want to, simply based on the fact that I felt guilty for saying no. Now, even though it still feels uncomfortable, I am able to say "No" when I am being asked to do things that simply do not feel right in my Soul because I KNOW that in agreeing, I would only be falling back into old belief patterns instead of upholding healthy boundaries put in place for my Highest Good. I know that my connection to myself and the foundational relationship I have built is to be honored, and those ego thoughts that continue to creep in are pushed to the back burner while I put my Soul first.

I have proved this to myself over and over, each time I make a decision to follow that inner nudge instead of the external opinion, each time I decide to trust in myself and my Divine wisdom we are all here with, each time I take those tiny steps forward in believing in myself regardless if no one else does, I am shown even more evidence, even more validation that my trust and belief in myself will never steer me wrong. My inner voice, my Higher wisdom slowly becomes louder and my ego voice, my inner critic, slowly becomes quieter and is no longer the one running the show.

This certainly did not happen overnight, I had a multitude of fears and belief systems to face and work through to get to this point, work that I am still doing and will continue to do because I never want to stop growing and up-leveling myself. However, the one fear that was my biggest obstacle to overcome was my fear of judgment and rejection. I know that this is a very common fear and one that likely holds most back from reaching their highest potential because it can be absolutely paralyzing and stop you right in your tracks. It WAS absolutely paralyzing, and it took me a long time to finally believe in myself enough to step through it and actually come out of the safety and security of my "spiritual closet".

My spiritual closet is how I refer to my former safe space, a community of like-minded people supporting and holding space for each other to investigate this journey into ourselves and navigate through the ups and downs of it. I realized that by me keeping all of my downloaded ideas and guidance of how I was supposed to help and support women written down in my phone for my eyes only, was actually an act of disservice to myself and the many women I am meant to support. I was in fact only dimming my Light, shrinking away into the background, and allowing this fear to dictate my actions and my life, instead of facing it head-on and shining my Light for others to see, and sharing what I was meant to share with this world.

I have realized that we are all our own unique Lights, our own unique Souls meant to attract only those that see our Light. I have realized that my fear of rejection was based on my programmed belief that I must change, or play small, or hide parts of myself in order to get everyone to like me when my actual truth is that not everyone WILL like me, and that is OK. That is a truth that I will continually work on, so that my belief in myself and my mission to help women transform their lives and experience these beautiful life changing shifts that I have, the WHY behind what I do, will ALWAYS override my old pattern of needing approval and acceptance from external sources outside of myself, and lead me back to my authentic truth in knowing that the only approval I will ever need is my own.

It was with that very truth that was shown to me, that deep belief in myself that what I am meant to share is so much more impactful and valuable than any limiting belief system, that I stepped out with shaking knees, a racing heart, and butterflies in my stomach into the unknown. Into the space of complete visibility and vulnerability, filled with those that had no idea who I actually was at a Soul level, those close to me that I kept the very heart of my being hidden from for so long, and those who had never met me, who would form their own opinions and judgments around my truth and what I am here to do. This was the VERY thing that had scared me the most, and so I held on to my belief in what I am here to do matters, and that in serving others I am serving myself and my Soul, and THAT is the feeling that rang true for me, the feeling I held on to every time I would press "post" on my public Facebook page talking about how I communicate with Angels, and every time I hit "Go Live" to speak about the spiritual insight I was guided to share. That feeling of absolute FREEDOM that I gave myself when I stopped allowing my fear of judgment and rejection to be the loudest voice I heard, and instead embraced the numerous encouraging comments and support that I had received from people who were inspired by me stepping out straight into the face of that fear, THAT feeling was absolutely priceless.

Being introduced to that knowing that I am always supported in ways I do not expect when I follow my truth, that knowing that finally, after a lifetime of people-pleasing and molding myself into someone that I thought I was supposed to be, of fitting in the box that I allowed others to put me in, that knowing that it was ok to just be me, was the very thing that would set me free. Free to be me in my truest, most authentic, unapologetic version of myself that I have ever been.

This crazy ride of a Soul journey that I have been on so far has been the most difficult and challenging path that I have ever faced, but one that I will be forever grateful for, as it has also shown me the true meaning of fulfillment, of peace from within, of happiness originating inside of me instead of from someone or something else, and of true deep unconditional love for myself that is still growing with each passing day, and each tiny decision that I make to honor myself and my Divine Soul, and I would not trade those experiences for anything.

SHANNON OLSEN

~

Shannon is an Angel Medium, Spiritual Mentor, Crystal Healer, and is the founder of her spiritual wellness business Vibrations of Light.

She communicates with a team of eight Angels to guide herself as well as her clients and has been on her own spiritual journey for many years now in which she is still growing, healing, and expanding. The feeling of fulfillment that comes when you are aligned with your Higher Self and your Soul's calling is just indescribable, and that is the reason behind Shannon's work.

Shannon helps women skyrocket their self worth to unlock the next level version of themselves who is empowered, fulfilled, inspired, bolder, wiser, and unstoppable by learning to tap into their Divine power so that they can find their unique path and purpose they are being guided to without the fear of judgment or disapproval from others.

Find Shannon here:
Facebook Page
https://www.facebook.com/vibrationsoflight444
Facebook Group
https://www.facebook.com/groups/spiritualsoulsisters
Instagram

https://www.instagram.com/shannonleaholsen/
Facebook Profile
https://www.facebook.com/profile.php?id=100005334468291
Email
vibrationsoflight444@gmail.com

3

ENCOUNTERS WITH STRANGERS: LEARNING IT'S SAFE TO BE ME

REGYNA CURTIS

In my earliest years, I remember playing in the dirt, laughing, rewriting my favorite stories into plays that generally starred me and made character-appropriate spaces for whoever would play along with me. I never wrote them down, but made them up as we went along which excited me and often annoyed my playmates. I made up friends when no one was available and created whole worlds to explore with whatever tools and spaces were accessible to me. I fought fiercely for animals and saw magic everywhere, but this changed a bit over time.

When school started, I showed up proud of knowing how to read and count well beyond 100 (thanks to my older sister!). I was received as far too much and quickly became a burden. I was bored at school and wanted to learn rather than play, but most of my classmates were still learning their alphabet. My parents refused to allow me to skip a grade because they felt I wouldn't fit in socially with the older classmates. I'm not sure why that ever was a concern, because I had always been drawn to adults and older children from whom I could learn more about the world.

I learned that I move too quickly and must slow down to be accepted.

In my elementary-aged years, the words *intuitive* and *empathic* did not yet hold any meaning. Instead, those who embodied those qualities were known as weird and there was an unspoken understanding that *perhaps they were dangerous, so better to keep your distance.*

Jewel Soul - Allergic to Electricity

The first "stranger" that I remember encountering was Jewel Soul. She lived a bit up the road from us in a cabin in the woods with no electricity. She had changed and chosen her own name; at least that's the story I remember. She had some kind of emergency and needed to use our telephone. This was long before the days of cell phones or even cordless phones, so she had to come into the house. She asked that we turn off the lights because she was allergic to electricity. She did not stay long and I recall her saying something about feeling the electricity as a burning sensation.

I learned that sensitive equals weird.

Bernie - The Mushroom Man

Then came Bernie. We lived on a mountain at this time, and he lived even further up the mountain, somewhere deep in the woods behind our house. You could sometimes see glimpses of his roofline in the winter when the trees had no leaves. He came to visit one day to share his bounty of wild mushrooms, as he had gathered more than he could eat. They were yellowish-orange and had a distinct musty smell and a pungent taste. I had been taught that only mushrooms from the store were edible. We ate them anyway.

I learned that the secret magic of the woods is shared through strangers.

Michael - Rocks Are People Too

Michael was eccentric. He and his family lived in our house before we did. He had placed large rocks in various places around the property, and there were gardens planted around them. He showed up one day unannounced to retrieve his lucky sheep's horn. He couldn't remember where he'd left it, but it was sure to still be in our house. I knew immediately where it was-tucked into the rafters in the basement. I'd seen it many times and wondered why it was there. Later he opened a rock museum, which I never visited but heard all about from my schoolmates. They described it as a bunch of ordinary rocks that were given names. I imagined them with googly eyes and names like people have. I was intrigued but told it was not a safe place for me to go.

I learned that seeing the world differently equals crazy.

Later in life, my encounters with strangers became more potent and elaborate. I had managed to stuff all of the weird and unusual parts of myself safely away, yet a new language began to emerge. I carefully steered clear of anything potentially dangerous that may contain or somehow be a portal into the worlds of the supernatural. However, I had a strong draw to personal development and holistic wellness. Eventually, these worlds would meet in the middle-directly inside of me.

A few weeks after I graduated college, I moved to Atlanta to start a new chapter. I had just left a relationship where I'd somehow lost myself and felt so detached from everything I had once identified as me. This led me into an interest in astrology and I created my natal chart for the first time. I returned to my journal practice and started drawing in my sketchbook again. I was determined to find my recognizable self yet I still felt she was very distant. There was something that wasn't quite fitting into place yet. There was still something that I needed to release.

At that time in my life, I bounced back and forth between leaning into my spiritual practices-writing in my journal, doing yoga, things like that-and running fiercely in the opposite direction. When I leaned in, I would see a definite opening and expansion which would then freak me out and send me running-contracting it all back in to take a pause before coming right back again-so it was no surprise then when the following happened.

Taylor's Grandmother - A Message From Beyond

I worked the midday shift at a preschool, so generally, I was there for the busiest part of the day when the 12 one-year-old toddlers filled the room. I enjoyed this job and have never felt more loved than during those days spent surrounded by those tiny newly landed souls. I needed them so much at that time.

One day, I worked the closing shift for my co-teacher. It was a rainy, chilly fall day-my favorite, and I had only a few kids left. I was in the process of bundling everyone up in their jackets and boots to head out to the playground for the remaining pickups. I loved all the babies, but there was one with whom I had a deeper bond. She would light up when she toddled into the room and always met me with a huge smile, sparkling eyes, and arms outstretched ready for a hug.

Usually, her mom picked her up but on this day, it was her dad and grandma. Her grandma was visiting from out of town so I'd never met her before and would never meet her again. Yet she would remain in my heart forever. They arrived just as I was zipping up the last of the jackets, so they exchanged only brief pleasantries, gathered their things, and we parted ways. They left out the front door as I daisy-chained out the back towards the playground with the rest of my tiny friends.

A few minutes passed on the playground, and then I felt her presence before I actually saw her. I turned around, and standing outside of the gate was the grandmother whom I'd just met.

"Oh, hi. Did you forget something?" I asked.

"No. I came back to deliver a message to you. I hope you don't find this strange but I had an overwhelming sense that you needed to hear this." she explained.

"Okay," I responded, not quite sure what else to say.

"If you don't take care of yourself," she said, "someone else is going to have to take care of you."

She looked me straight in the eyes as she delivered this message with a stern kindness that felt quite familiar.

"Thank you" I replied.

I felt her message land deeply in my heart and she was gone as quickly as she'd arrived.

That night. I laid in bed before sleeping and sent a message to my own grandmother who had died many years earlier. I'd been too afraid to receive her in spirit form after she died and had fallen asleep most nights feeling her presence yet asking her not to appear because the thought of it frightened me too much.

I told her that I missed her and loved her and was ready to receive her in my dreams if she were willing to meet me there. She arrived in my dream as a phone call. I couldn't see her but I could hear her voice and feel her love. My great-grandmother was there with her as well. We had a normal conversation about what was happening in my life like we'd had countless times when she was alive, but before the dream ended, she told me that she is always there when I need her and that I can call her anytime. A new chapter had begun.

I learned that strangers sometimes speak the truth that I don't have words for.

My Mysterious Waitress

Several years later; it was Halloween night. My bank account had less than $30 in it. I'd driven from Atlanta to Asheville in my co-workers' car through the twisting mountains and curves. I was tired and hungry and filled with adrenaline.

I sat in the parking lot shared by my hotel, an Outback Steakhouse, and a local barbecue joint. I craved a nice dinner; perhaps a glass of wine. It had been a hell of a day. There was a battle going on in my mind. One voice encouraged me to go get the dinner I wanted and another ran numbers and encouraged me to start the car back up, drive to a grocery store, and buy something cheaper. As this debate continued, a third voice entered and the others became silent.

"It will be okay. Go in."

My mind was made up and my body started moving. Before I knew it, I'd entered the Outback and was having some kind of out-of-body experience. I had two realities occurring simultaneously. I was aware of my thoughts and actions and also experiencing them from another consciousness that was much clearer and very confident.

I'll just sit at the bar-in and out quickly. I'll order light, no wine.

"Welcome to the Outback would you like to sit at the bar or a booth?"

"A booth please."

Wait, where did that come from?

We walked by the bar and she sat me in a booth big enough to fit 10 people. *"This is nice,"* I thought and I settled in, scanning the menu for something cheaper than what I really wanted. The waitress sat down in the booth across from me. She was very kind and looked me straight in the eyes when she spoke to me like we knew each other well. I ended up ordering exactly what my body was craving and before she left she asked in a manner more like a statement than a question

"...and what kind of wine did you want with that?"

"Shiraz please."

I floated back into my body for a moment and panicked.

Regyna-what the hell are you doing?!?

The inner accountant appeared again and reassured me that my overdraft would kick in to cover my bill and that payday was the following day, and... my meal arrived. I savored it. I have no idea how long I sat there that night. The restaurant was nearly empty. Just one man sitting at the bar. No one else in sight. It was quiet and dark and cozy. It was exactly what I was looking for.

Eventually, the dreaded moment came. The waitress arrived with my check. She sat once again across from me in the giant booth, placed the check on the table enclosed in a black booklet, and neatly and casually sat with her hands crossed on top of it in front of her. She asked how my meal was and listened patiently as I thanked her for everything.

"How about some dessert?" she asked.

"No thank you."

I didn't need to push it, and I was already quite satisfied with my meal as it was.

"Another glass of wine then?"

She carefully walked me through my options. Not at all as an upsell but very genuinely wanting to be sure that I'd had all I needed. She was in no rush. The restaurant was nearly empty. I could sense that she had something more to say. Still with her hands crossed slightly over the bill, she asked if it was okay to share something with me.

"Yes."

"You are very loved," she said.

This took me a bit by surprise. I know she said some other things but I can't remember them exactly anymore. She was calm and confident in her delivery. Before she left she looked me straight in the eyes again and asked

"Are you sure you don't want anything else?"

As I answered that I was truly fine, she said "good" and pulled the check closer to her.

"Your bill has already been paid."

My eyes shot quickly to the bar where I'd seen the one man there eating earlier but the seats were all empty.

"She has already left."

She? Huh? ... Grandma. Thank you.

The thoughts clearly and lovingly flooded through my mind and heart.

As she stood up to leave, she smiled and wished me a beautiful evening, and reminded me one more time that I am loved.

The next morning my good friend who is a medium called saying "I've been thinking about you." As we chatted, she began casually asking me about details from my early childhood home; the one I lived in with my grandparents. Before I could figure out what was happening enough to freak myself out, I realized that she was channeling my grandmother. I had avoided this moment-actively pushing it away for nearly a decade since her passing because I was scared, and because I was sure she was disappointed in me or angry at me for some stupid things I'd done as a child.

The reunion was anything but scary. It was heartwarming and actually quite fun at times. When we hung up the phone I felt lighter and more sure than ever that she had somehow orchestrated the purchase of my dinner the night before.

Phew!, I thought. *Okay, so maybe she wasn't mad at me after all.*

Almost on cue as that thought completed, I received a text from my friend with a description of an image that she just couldn't get out of her head. Her description immediately brought me to tears because it was representative of exactly the reason I had feared contact all of those years. Along with it came a message from my grandmother about how she loves me no matter what and that she always knew and never cared.

"You are very loved."

I learned that I am deeply loved and supported and that my inner compass will not steer me wrong.

Regyna Curtis (Me) - Soul Wisdom Mentor

I've had many encounters with strangers throughout my life that have formed and reformed my belief patterns. These lessons have come through the reactions of others in the moment as well as how they've stayed with me, continuing to help me reflect on and adjust my perspective over time.

Several years ago, after an intense but beautiful and inspiring healing experience with two strangers, I consciously embarked on a journey. This moment marked the beginning of a new level of exploration for me into my intuitive gifts and ultimately resulted in the creation of my business, Atmaitri, where I support soul wisdom explorers along their journey of evolution. I've encountered many teachers who've helped me to identify, deepen my understanding of, and experiment with how to work with my unique gifts. These teachers were a catalyst for my intentional pursuit of becoming fluent in the language of my soul wisdom.

A huge part of my life education has come through my personal connections, yet some of the most potent insights and biggest transformations have come with the assistance of complete strangers showing up in my life to help usher them in. There was a time when I attracted odd people and situations. They stood out to me as odd because they weren't happening to other people as far as I could see. Now, these people are my friends, colleagues, and mentors, and these situations are part of my everyday normal existence.

Many would call this a spiritual awakening. I believe that we have spiritual awakenings frequently, just as we are born and then awaken each day. We are connected with our spirituality, like a rebirth, and then awaken continuously each time we expand or deepen our awareness, unlocking new gifts.

Each of the encounters I've shared here has been an invitation for me to open further, explore deeper, and trust with vulnerability and compassion the wisdom that exists within me. It is not always easy to allow your authentic ways of knowing and being to be seen by others. We are each different than many and similar to some; a unique recipe that makes us exactly who we are. Becoming fluent in our own soul wisdom helps build the road of acceptance and conscious living for all of us. We inherently provide permission to everyone we encounter as we show up authentically as ourselves.

Stepping into this role of soul wisdom leadership means that I consciously create my life through the guidance of this wisdom. I share it openly along with the journey of how I've arrived here and hope that others may find their own internal guidance systems more easily and share their gifts with confidence and compassion as I do.

I am a soul wisdom leader. I lead my life guided by the wisdom of my soul and support and empower others to do the same. It is not my intent to teach you how to do things like me. It is my mission to encourage you to do them like you.

REGYNA CURTIS

~

Regyna Curtis is an internationally bestselling author on the subjects of spirituality and creativity. Her stories take you on an adventure of self-discovery, weaving insights from her personal journey throughout the physical and spiritual realms with her work as a Soul Wisdom Mentor.

With over 40 years of experience living as an intuitive being, Regyna has achieved fluency in the language of her soul. She is an expert in interpreting soul wisdom languages and uses this to support and empower individuals to find confidence and clarity in living their most authentically soul-aligned lives.

A natural storyteller with a gift for relaying complex concepts in relatable, useful, and entertaining ways, Regyna will keep you on the edge of your seat, curious to know what happens next. She is a sought-after podcast guest, speaker, and workshop facilitator, founder of her soul-led business Atmaitri, host of the Soul Wisdom Exchange podcast, an art channel, and an enthusiastic world traveler.

Learn More on Her Website: www.atmaitri.com
Get Your Own Channeled Artwork: https://www.etsy.com/shop/atmaitri
Listen to the Soul Wisdom Exchange Podcast: Streamed live on Facebook and YouTube and available on Podbean and Apple Podcasts

Connect on Social Media: @Atmaitri on Instagram, Facebook, YouTube, and @regynaatmaitri on TikTok

Network on LinkedIn: https://www.linkedin.com/in/regyna-curtis-1472b47/

4

TAKING A STAND FOR ME
CHANIN ZELLNER

I felt him get into my bed and snuggle up behind me, squeezing me VERY close to him. He was only wearing his underwear, and I felt every part of him. I do not remember what happened after that, but it horribly impacted the next 45 years of my life.

I was between four to six years old when this male authority figure molested me - I was not his only target. Every time I saw him, I was expected to hug him, and he would always manage to touch the sides of my boobs. Eventually, I figured out a way to hug him so he could not do that anymore.

This story is not an uncommon one. Millions of children have been molested or raped by a relative or family friend. Like so many families, mine seemingly chose to ignore what was happening. Many people who have been sexually traumatized block out the details from their conscious minds, but the emotional and physical effects can last a lifetime.

I was your stereotypical middle-child. Not only that, but I was also the middle cousin. The older kids did not want to play with me, and I did not want to play with the younger kids. I was always craving attention and affection. Yet, because of the trauma I endured, I would not allow people to get close to me, emotionally or physically. I desperately wanted to be hugged but would avoid it if I could as I did not want to be touched.

This desire for love and attention also caused me to be ridiculously competitive! It was so bad I would cheat at board games with my younger sister and cousins and eventually they did not want to play with me. This set me up to be an oversensitive "crybaby" for much of my life. The family joke was – it was not a holiday until Chanin was crying.

At an early age, my need for love contributed to me becoming a people pleaser and overachiever who needed external validation of my worth. I excelled in school, even skipping two grades. I remember when I told an uncle that I skipped second grade he shamed me for bragging. So, I learned that being successful was something to be ashamed about.

The molestation I endured as a young child was not the only time someone violated my body and my personal space. One of my vivid memories of being violated happened when I was nine. There was a boy in my class who liked me. During recess one day, a group of boys dragged me to the bleachers at the end of the field so the boy could kiss me. I do not recall if he actually did, but when I returned to the classroom, the teacher condemned me in front of everyone for being late. It was extremely embarrassing and humiliating as everyone in the class knew what happened.

The sexual trauma also caused me to be EXTREMELY self-conscious about my body. As early as eleven years old, I would not wear shirts that showed my bra straps or were slightly see-through. I feared drawing unwanted attention to myself as I had learned I could be harmed because of my appearance.

I lived in a world of constant internal conflict. On one hand, I wanted to be seen, loved, and validated. Yet, I also wanted to be as invisible as possible. As time passed, my confidence and self-esteem got squashed. I avoided trying anything new. I was TERRIFIED to speak up in class or express my opinions. I usually stayed inside my comfort zone because I was safe there. While there were additional reasons for this need for safety, I would do all I could to be invisible. I absolutely did not want people looking at me, judging me, or potentially harming me in some way.

By the time I was sixteen, my need to fly under the radar swung the opposite way. I adopted a punk rocker persona. I colored my hair and wore gaudy jewelry and attention-getting clothing. I no longer wanted to be invisible. I wanted attention – negative or positive! In hindsight, I realized that I was rejecting people so they could not reject me first. I was not going to give them the opportunity to NOT see or love me. It was my unconscious way of maintaining control and staying safe.

When I went to college, I rebelled against society even more. In my freshman year, I gained thirty pounds by Thanksgiving. I became loud and obnoxious. I developed an extremely unhealthy drinking problem to the point I was drinking alone, blacking out regularly, sometimes waking up in unfamiliar places. I was extremely lonely and ended up alienating people because of my drinking and my attitude. The depression that had started in high school deepened. Moreover, I was on academic probation because I was not attending classes. My life was a nightmare.

One night while hanging out with girlfriends at a bar on campus, we were invited to an off-campus party. My girlfriends backed out, but I knew one of the guys, so I decided to go. When we arrived at the guys' house, one of them mentioned how they all were going to "have a turn with me". Reality hit me very quickly. Thankfully, after a lot of screaming and kicking, they actually let me leave. My guardian angel was definitely working overtime to keep me alive that year! I did not return to college.

When I was nineteen my parents kicked me out of their house because I would not follow their rules. I moved in with my boyfriend who I had known for three weeks. At this point, I was a complete wreck. I was still depressed, experimenting with drugs, drinking too much, driving drunk every weekend, and struggling to keep a job. And my boyfriend had his own emotional baggage that I was entirely unprepared to manage.

My dad passed away in 1990 at the age of 46, and this was a tremendous blow to my family. While he certainly had flaws, he was my hero. My boyfriend and I married seven months later. It was an explosive marriage that completely obliterated any self-esteem I had prior to meeting him. I had no self-love. I was depressed, pessimistic, and insanely jealous, controlling, and possessive. I had such a fear of rejection and abandonment that I would throw a fit if he wanted to hang out with his friends. He became emotionally and verbally abusive due to his own issues.

We had two young boys and we were struggling financially. We got suckered into a side business idea of buying products wholesale and then selling them at a discount. We racked up immense debt that we could not pay and eventually declared bankruptcy. We lost a daughter who died in utero at 16 weeks. I had told my husband numerous times that if I were not pregnant, I would leave him. So, after she died, I carried immense guilt for decades. Thankfully, a friend helped me realize that the way he was treating me was abusive. I subconsciously believed I deserved the mistreatment, and I was so beaten down I did not believe I could survive on my own. I believed I was a worthless loser who was undeserving of love or happiness. But I did leave him with my friend's support.

And then I met my next husband who was even MORE abusive. I was never good enough. Nothing I did was ever right. No matter what I did to try to "make" him love me, I was not worthy of it. We had a daughter, so leaving my second husband seemed impossible with three children to help support. And at that time, I was extremely religious and believed if I divorced him, I would go to hell. More guilt and shame! Eventually, I got the courage to leave once I realized I was not doing my children any favors by staying in the marriage. When I told our 6-year-old daughter her dad and I were getting a divorce, she responded, "At least you won't be fighting anymore." That sealed the decision.

At this point in my life, I was full of shame, guilt, regret, and embarrassment. I was certain I had deserved all the mistreatment I had experienced in my life. I did not love myself. I did not believe God loved me. I was not worthy. I had done and said so many horrible things in my life. There were SO many times in my life I wanted to DIE. Many times, I would be in my car at a red light and considered driving into traffic in the hopes I would be killed.

I took anti-depressants off and on for 20 years. I had chronic low back pain since I was eight and I had developed fibromyalgia and anxiety during my second marriage. But during all of this, I KNEW at a SOUL level there was something important for me to do in this lifetime.

During these tumultuous years, I explored numerous self-help courses and books. I learned about the "concept" of energy and the power of our minds. I was exposed to the idea that our thoughts create our realities. I kept grasping at straws trying to find the CURE for what ailed me. I wanted to know WHY I was always struggling and WHY I kept attracting people who hurt me. I wanted to be HAPPY!

And then I met my current husband. He had two kids of his own and was stable, kind, and caring. I knew at a soul level when I first met him that he was SAFE. We had a lot of challenges as a blended family. A LOT. And all my kids had their own struggles we worked through. But my husband was an answer to a prayer. I needed someone who would support me no matter what and who was committed to his own evolution. I was still dealing with depression, anxiety, low self-esteem, and little self-love, and I was CERTAIN he would leave me too. Who would put up with someone like me? I certainly did not deserve to be loved after all the mistakes I had made. I used to joke that if you looked up the word "guilt" in the dictionary you would see my picture.

We got married in Sedona, Arizona in 2008. I had created a four-part ceremony that included different faiths. We got married by a shaman under Snoopy's Rock while wearing hiking boots. In hindsight, I am still astounded my husband agreed to it!

After we got married, I went to a counselor named Mavis Karn. She told me the wisest thing I had ever heard. "We all do the best we can with the knowledge we have at the time." That was a HUGE light bulb moment for me! It still took another ten years for me to TRULY know what that statement meant, but it was a catalyst to tremendous changes that would happen within me.

In 2010 I started a bookkeeping company. This resulted in a HUGE boost to my self-esteem and self-worth! People valued me! People LOVED how I was able to help them! It brought me such joy! And I participated in a networking group where I HAD to talk to people and give presentations and even meet strangers in public places. This was TREMENDOUS growth for me as I had lived most of my life living with the fear of being harmed, judged, and ridiculed. My company grew rapidly, and I eventually had four employees. I was successful! I apparently DID deserve success and love! But I still lived on a roller coaster of reactive and often irrational emotions.

And then the Universe brought me to Alison J. Kay in 2017. She and I were in the same high school class although we did not know each other. Thirty years later I found her on Facebook through mutual friends and I joined her free Facebook group. A month later, I woke up and my neck was STUCK, causing horrendous pain. I went to multiple doctors, but I did not improve much. So, I started my internet research. I had heard of chakras and determined that I had a throat chakra blockage. I then went to three different energy workers who told me the same thing.

A month later I attended Alison's free monthly call, and not knowing who I was, she chose me to help. She diagnosed me with a throat chakra problem, and I was sold! I TOOK A STAND FOR ME! While I knew I had some "issues", I had NO idea about the depth of trauma I had trapped in my body. My main purpose for joining her paid program was to get help starting a non-profit to help veterans. I never imagined the path I would eventually take because of Alison and her Vibrational UPgrade™ System.

Through working with Alison for over 3 1/2 years I completely transformed from a woman who lived in constant emotional and physical pain to one who can unconditionally love herself and everyone else. Through energy medicine and applied mindfulness coaching, we healed most of the trauma that had caused so much suffering. The journey has been SO CHALLENGING AND PAINFUL at times. I have cried an ocean's worth of tears! But now I can choose JOY and LOVE no matter what is happening around me!

I had NO idea how the sexual trauma had impacted my life! I learned that when we have trauma, our minds can develop false beliefs and get wired to believe that danger is everywhere. My mind had developed incredible defense mechanisms to keep me safe from harm. It took Alison and I years to break them down and rewire my brain to believe that the Universe is FOR me and not AGAINST me.

I also learned in-depth about how emotional reactions to trauma get stored in our bodies and block our chakras which help disperse our vital life-force energy. These energetic blockages can create illness, disease, and chronic pain. With all the transformation I have done, I no longer have fibromyalgia, depression, and chronic pain. And if I do have a new pain occur, I know to delve into what emotions I am holding onto that need acknowledged and released.

I now know I am a DIVINE being, created in the image of Source. There is no separation. I KNOW that I AM LOVE, LOVED and LOVABLE. I do not have to seek approval and validation from others. I am worthy of love and success because the spark of Source is WITHIN ME. I now believe that I can accomplish anything I truly set my mind to!

I believe in UNITY. As we are all comprised of energy, we are all connected. We are ONE consciousness. There is no need for competition and comparing. We each have our unique gifts, talents, and experiences to share with the world in the way that only WE can. There is NO ONE else like YOU! You are needed just as you are, imperfectly perfect.

I KNOW that our thoughts, actions, and words create our realities. We are NOT subject to the whim of fate. When we KNOW this and live in a state of trust and surrender while taking inspired action, we CAN have our heart's desires.

I also have accepted everything that has happened in my life. I have gratitude for EVERY experience. Every person was a teacher. Every experience was a lesson. And it all helped mold me into who I am NOW. And I love me! I have managed to forgive and even develop compassion for the people who harmed me knowing that at some point in their lives, they were harmed too. They behaved the best they could with the knowledge they had at the time. This is an EXTREMELY powerful place to be.

It is my passion and Soul's mission to help YOU know that YOU are an infinite Divine being. YOU deserve to experience an abundance of love, peace, happiness, and success. You are NOT what has happened to you. Those are just moments in time, and they do not define your Soul's essence. You ARE love. You ARE loved. You ARE lovable. You are needed on this planet! It is SAFE to be YOU. You are allowed to speak your truth!

It is time for you to heal too and remember who YOU are at a Soul level. You have a wonderful purpose that only YOU can fulfill! It is time for you to take a stand for YOU – for you are LOVED!

CHANIN ZELLNER

∼

Chanin Zellner is an International best-selling collaborative author, a speaker, successful entrepreneur, and professionally trained energy medicine practitioner "extraordinaire" whose soul's mission is to share unconditional love and joy with the world to help create Heaven on Earth.

She has spent the last three decades immersed in the study of metaphysics, spirituality, and personal development. Using her ever-increasing psychic gifts, Chanin accurately identifies and helps heal her clients' emotional blocks, traumas, and false beliefs that keep them from creating the lives they desire.

Chanin has a fiery passion for helping people move beyond their sexual trauma as she has triumphed over the effects of her own trauma. She is empathetic, compassionate, and loving and has a remarkable ability to emanate a sense of peace, safety, and love to everyone who is ready to receive it.

Connect with Chanin at www.thelightvessel.com.
Receive free energy medicine healing here:
https://www.youtube.com/watch?v=d9ngUqILkMs

5

WISDOM BETWEEN THE LEAVES
CHARLOTTE DE JAEGHER

You think the only people who are people
Are the people who look and think like you
But if you walk the footsteps of a stranger
You'll learn things you never knew,
you never knew.
Colors of the Wind - Judy Kuhn

It is 5 am, and I hear a loud ringing noise. Ring! Ring It was my alarm giving me the message to wake up. I didn't want to listen to it, but I had to. A little bit confused, I opened my eyes. It was still dark outside. Other travelers of the hostel where I stayed were also waking up slowly to get ready. As we were far away from our home country, we only had each other and became very close. We carpooled daily to the village's station, Blenheim, north of the southern island of New Zealand. Little vans picked us up, driving us to different destinations. Not many words were spoken in the van, as we're all so tired of working ten to twelve hours daily. As I stepped out of the van, the sun was rising. The light revealed a fantastic landscape with hills, a vineyard, and a breathtaking sky with warm colors.

It was time to work before I picked apples, but now I picked grapes. It might seem like something straightforward and easy to do, but as a matter of fact, it was the most demanding physical job I have ever done in my life. I love learning and searching for deeper meaning in my jobs, such as sports teacher, health/life coach, school care coördinator, and business owner. I didn't experience picking grapes as a mental challenge, and not being able to challenge my mind made the job challenging for me in a different way. However, I also managed to find deeper meaning in picking fruits and learned to appreciate and respect the simple things in life more. So how did I get up here?

Months before working on the vineyard in New Zealand, I lived in Gent. Not much seemed to flow back then in my life, job, financial situation, relationship, low self-esteem, dealing with death, basically a lack of direction and purpose in my life. I was fading out slowly under depressing thoughts. I experienced a lack of knowledge of dealing healthily with difficult situations. I did what society, family, and friends expected of me. In this process, I could not recognize my heart's desires, and I was unaware of the signs of my instincts.

I felt broken inside until the day I discovered the concept of a working holiday. You get a work visa which allows you to work and travel for a specific time in some countries. When the dark days in my life were draining out my energy, I needed to go away, and so I did. Full of adrenaline, I booked my ticket to the other side of the world all by myself. Finally, it slowly dawns on me, What am I doing? It was not the first time I had gone to the other side of the world. Working three months as a sports teacher as an intern at a primary school in Costa Rica was a deep, insightful experience and created a desire for more. I realized this was not the end on the last day of that journey. A tear rolled over my smiling lips while I watched the breathtaking scenery.

Breathing in the fresh air and feeling the warm sunlight on my skin gave me energy. I have already worked at three different picking companies, and now it was my first day at one of the Maoris. The Maoris are an interesting race of people who live in New Zealand and the Cook Islands even long before Europeans arrived. In New Zealand, the Maori people maintain a strong culture. Unlike the other picking companies I worked for, they were so lovely and warm to the other workers and me. Picking grapes is not just randomly jumping around and picking one when you feel like it. Instead, there are different systems of how to pick and what to select at a particular time.

A common rule in those companies is that we always have to be with two people on each side of the grape bush. This time I had to pick with a granny Maori. We briefly saw each other before we stood on the other side of the bush filled with golden juicy grapes. She looked young for her age and had a vivid glow. I was amazed that she could do this hard work at her age with a smile.

We cut the best grapes from the bushes and drop them into the baskets most of the time. But today, we cut the rotten ones out of the grapes. I opened the scissors to cut and repeatedly saw the rotten grapes fall on the ground. Then, perfectionistic and a little insecure, I checked if I didn't cut the good grapes even if they already fell on the earth. I needed to move on, but I focused too much on a reality that belonged now to the past. On something I could not change anymore.

After a few hours, the granny Maori told me how she grew up while we were picking grapes. I was so fascinated when she said to me that she was born somewhere deep in the jungle in the north of the northern island of New Zealand. She talked about her eight siblings and growing up in the wilderness. Even though their family didn't have much money, they supported each other and were happy together. I loved listening to her stories. As a city girl, I never imagined growing up deep in nature with so many siblings. I was fascinated by the idea that her reality was completely different than mine. I kept asking questions to learn more about how different the world could be. So the meaning of 'normal' was entirely different for us, yet it was the same word. We would envision something different with that same word, which created an opportunity to learn. At this moment, I realized the power of change by making other decisions. I felt strong and free by that thought. I don't have to live a life based on a low energy level. It became clearer that I could create a lifestyle that gives me energy in balance with inner peace with that thought; I didn't realize it, but a seed for founding my company, Arasari Lifestyle, was planted.

The position of the sun changed as time went by. We worked and talked for hours about culture, nature, relationships, childhood, dreams, and work. Even though picking grapes wasn't the most fun job to do, that time with the granny Maori felt magical. I could only see a glimpse of her presence through the grape bushes, but her stories and messages were clear and resonating with my hunger and curiosity for knowledge and her profound insights.

The light was flickering through the leaves of the bush when I heard the wise words with a warm voice: 'Let go of what you don't need, my dear.' The granny Maori noticed that I sometimes stood still for a second. The moment she said it, I knew she was not only talking about the rotten grapes, which I was checking lying on the earth. 'Live in the moment and accept that it's ok to let the moment go to make space for new experiences' was coming through between the leaves, reaching my heart.

Shifting between the shadow and the light

I love it when the beauty of the sunlight comes through the leaves and conjures a smile on my face. So, after hours and hours cutting the grapes, I learned to work on an automated pilot. It gave me mental space to observe the breathtaking scenery's spectacle of light and shadow. But then, my mind wandered off far out of New Zealand to Sydney, Australia, with its beautiful harbor. I've done an internship at a health coaching fitness in Double Bay with outstanding coaches. One day while creating marketing content, I felt perplexed about the next steps in my life. Anxious, I wanted and needed answers.

I learned during my journey that it's about the questions, not the answers. One of the coaches gave me space to have a pity party, confronted me by looking at my actual shadow on the ground and using it as a metaphor. While looking at the shadow, she invited me to say all my worries aloud. After that, I turned my face towards the sun and took in the warmth and light. At that moment, I had to formulate questions that would give me a different outcome. For example: Why am I bad at this? Adapt to 'How can I do better?' Thoughts influence emotions; this will be visible in daily habits and the quality of our lives. My train of thought broke when suddenly I heard a bird singing at the vineyard — I smiled, looking back at that memory.

Cut, let go, cut, let go — While my hands were doing the work, my mind drifted to the moment this wild adventure began. It was a chaotic night in my apartment in Belgium. Two great friends stayed over to help me pack and brought me to the airport. I was confused and scared, but their generous and loving support got me through the gate. I learned later in my journey that I needed to be scared first before I could be brave. It was one challenging step I took of millions to come. I hugged my lovely friends goodbye with a too-heavy backpack. There's a saying by the Triprebel Manifesto; 'We travelers own what we can carry.' I was used to having a material mindset and holding on to physical and emotional baggage. So I started my transforming journey with twenty-five kg luggage, divided over two backpacks. I had the ideal belief that the more I carry my stuff, the stronger I'll become. So I don't need to let go of stuff even though I have to face the consequences, like having back pain or feeling mentally drained. It was ok because I thought what doesn't kill you makes you stronger. I was pushing, in reality, my boundaries mentally and physically too close to the limit, with an unhealthy mindset.

The light shimmers in my eyes, and a sound travels between the leaves toward me, making me snap out of my thoughts. "It's not because you can carry it that you have to.' The words of the Granny Maori coming through the leaves of the grape bush hit me deeply. I must have told her about my backpack and parts of my journey. She was correct; It means that it's ok to be strong as it is ok not to be.

However, I'm carrying actual baggage on my back, and the emotional baggage I have in my mind slowly broke me. I needed to live this life lesson vividly to understand what it meant to feel gravity pulling me down. I could have cried, complained, and resisted the reality at those moments, but this time I didn't. I couldn't escape the fact that what brought me in that situation was holding on to what I don't genuinely need. Next to this, I realized that the only thing between me and crashing to the ground was my iron will not give up and focus on my goals to survive and thrive.

Many people I crossed and shared paths with helped me (un)consciously to reflect on life lessons I couldn't see. The granny Maori's message gave me the insight to see more clearly and helped me connect the dots.'Let go of the baggage that you don't need.'

Stepping out of the shadows to shine and create a significant impact

A great leader learns from the darkest moments and steps out of their shadows. This leader lights the path to guide those who've lost their way. In their turn, the people who found their path can also step out of the shadows to shine and show more people the path of raising themselves to higher awareness. What a great leader does is raise awareness and create more leaders.

This chapter I wrote to honor my cousin, David Impens (01.04.1991 - 19.10.2021).

He passed away searching for a path covered with light of justice and freedom. Unfortunately, he didn't find the support and guidance in the western society of materialistic blindness, judgment, and shadows of a closed mindset for those who don't look or think the same. The 'system' didn't see him for who he was or could be because his light and his differences blinded them. He got lost in the shadows to fit in a society that wasn't willing to meet him halfway. He was an open, athletic, loving, caring dreamer who needed a warm, supportive community besides his loving family to guide him. This is an example of where 'The System' failed and where we need to wake up.

Rise to listen to the needs of those who ask for help and take action towards their and your needs. Let David's passing away be an inspiration to all of us to step up, speak up, for what's right, for protecting our boundaries, for respecting the boundaries of others, for creating a world where the shadows of judgments fade away in the light of support and acceptance of what is different.

I also wrote this story to inspire leaders to create a tremendous positive impact by raising awareness with an open, curious, and loving mindset to enhance the quality of life. Growing in your personal development is crucial to experience inner peace, which is essential to improve life quality. Step out of your comfort zone and connect with a stranger in a way that feels good for you both. Leave the shadow of judgment behind and learn the things you need to know.

Everyone, ready to follow their heart, support, and guide others to help them grow and raise awareness that they can be leaders. This can go from a world leader, CEO, manager to a teacher, a mother, a father, a scout leader, a friend, and a lover.

Walk with me in the footsteps of a stranger and learn the things you need to know.

Let's be open and face the truth about where we failed and where we can do better, where we can raise our standards. Then, let's take action towards those needs with an open, curious, and loving mindset.

> *I've been a warrior, and I know why*
> *I've been given the torch of light*
> *To walk in the darkness of the night*
> *Years we fought for this freedom*
> *Years I thought I had the wisdom*
> *Now I see with new eyes*
> *From this truth, I cannot hide*
> *I have to believe I'm here*
> *To make a difference without fear*
> *Of being seen or heard*
> *Like the bird who flies at night*
> *Like the lion, strong and fierce*
> *Like the whale singing*
> *I'd like to be bringing peace*
> *To you, to me, to you*
> Into the wild - Shylah Ray Sunshine

You might not imagine how enriching a story from someone with a different point of view, and life experience can be. So I invite you to go and explore with an open, curious, and positive mindset the reality of a stranger or acquaintance without judgment.

Gratitude Is the attitude.

I shared or crossed my path with many strangers, and I'm **grateful** for all that I've learned by their differences compared to me. Furthermore, I am **thankful** to see some of those *strangers become great friends* or enrich life with lessons, insights, or even beautiful experiences which will last a lifetime.

I use these experiences as <u>supporting metaphors</u> of letting go, stepping up, and shifting the mindset to help me remember these essential lessons, which help me learn, heal and grow. It inspires me to see, reignite, and share the magic that this life has to offer.

For example, the too-heavy back reminds me of the material-focused mindset transformed by a positive personal needs fulfilling attitude. But, of course, a materialistic economy conditions us to buy more. Still, it's important to remember to think for yourself by asking whether this resonates with what I need and believe?

Another example is: 'Cut the grapes and let go, repetitively. This is a reminder to let go of what no longer serves you to move forward. The grapes can stand for a job that makes you unhappy, a relationship where your worth isn't acknowledged, or even little things like clothes you're not wearing for years. There are many more examples, but you get the idea.

Last but not least, the shift to turn your body/ attitude from the shadow/ negative mindset towards the light/ positive mindset. Instead of focusing on what's pulling you down when challenging circumstances happen, shift your attention towards the possibilities. I invite you to dream wild and big, set goals, break them down into practical steps and take action towards them to create an extraordinary life that makes your eyes sparkle.

> *"The only limits you have,*
> *are the limits you believe you have."*
> Wayne Dyer

Supporting metaphors are like imaginary stones. They helped me, but they can help you too. You can create and use it anytime and anywhere. They can help you find your way back when you've lost it, like in the story of Hansel and Gretel. Losing your way can mean feeling stressed or burned out. These imaginary stones can support you in this lifelong process of learning, healing, growing, and transforming.

Did you know that a great way to spend your time and energy is being **grateful** for what you have and appreciate in your life? We can express it by saying it to people through words or gestures. Next to writing, there're many more ways to express this warm energy of being grateful. What resonates the most with you? It's a reliable way to create a healthy mindset by focusing on what gives you and others a good or great feeling. I would like to thank my partner, friends, family, ancestors, and those beautiful souls I crossed paths with and who inspired me to learn, heal, grow and transform.

Arasari Lifestyle, transforming strategies and coaching.

Dealing with difficult situations that give you stress, make you angry, sad, or burn out can feel like falling every time again. But, instead, what you want is to feel more energy, passion, and inner peace. It is like a hundred times, falling and struggling to get up that hundred and one times. At Arasari lifestyle, I help you make that step to get up and move forward a lot easier by offering support where needed and offering science-based knowledge, tips, raising your independence in an empowering and fun way.

Thank you for your time and energy connecting with my story. Feel free to let me know where this story resonates with you or what you get out of it. See my autobiography for my contact info. I'm looking forward to connecting with you! Pura Vida, it means in Spanish Pure Life, refers to a phrase encapsulating the culture of Costa Rica.

CHARLOTTE DE JAEGHER

Raising awareness holistically, improving the quality of life, and traveling are great passions of Charlottes. She travelled 1- 1/2 years solo and is the proud founder of Arasari Lifestyle, where she guides people to design a lifestyle they love and helps them deal with stress.

She became a certified teacher, health, life, and movement coach with a tremendous passion for education through her determination. Her many talents and warm intentions shine through her career. They have led to various opportunities for her to work as a corporate wellness manager, community creator, school-care coordinator, and studies psychology.

Charlotte was born in Belgium and is also known as Charlotte El Casador. Like the Arasari bird, she's playful, social, joyful, and has a free spirit.

Her goal is to encourage and inspire you to adapt to an open and curious mindset and take passion-based actions.

You can learn more about Charlotte and connect with her by visiting her website: https://arasari-lifestyle.com/Hello

6

FINDING MY AUTHENTIC SELF

KRISTEN TOSCANO

"Your authentic self goes beyond what you do for a living, what possessions you own, or who you are to someone (mom, brother, girlfriend). It is who you are at your deepest core. It is about being true to yourself through your thoughts, words, and actions, and having these three areas match each other. When we aren't in touch with our authentic self, it's easy to go into "people pleasing" mode and do and say things based off of what is expected of us, or based off of social and peer pressure." ~Jennifer Foust, Ph.D., M.S. LPC., Director of the Center for Growth

We all have a blueprint that guides us to understand our authentic selves. It's in exploring the themes of our blueprint that we grow and expand. But it's also in this exploration that we can sometimes get stuck when we don't understand these themes and how we energetically interact with the world around us. These misunderstandings can lead us to make judgments about ourselves that keep us from leaning into who we truly are and can lead us to take things personally when we're just feeling the energetic themes at play in an interaction.

When we look at our Human Design BodyGraph, we see the themes that are part of our soul curriculum on one side and our human/life story on the other. It's in the dance between these themes where we become wise and in fully expressing ourselves through these archetypal themes that we fulfill our purpose. Sometimes we find alignment on our own through our experiences, paying attention to the cues and clues from the Universe, and sometimes the Universe wakes us up with a less than gentle nudge that shifts our course to bring us closer to alignment and our souls' curriculum.

As a kid, math and science came easy to me, which I now see aligns with the logical way my mind works — Channel 63-4 defining my Head and Ajna Centers. Tapping into this natural ability to recognize patterns and use them to predict future outcomes worked well for me for a long time because it allowed me to fit into societal expectations of achievement and success. And it was reinforced with praise and recognition from all directions and kept me from dealing with criticism when things didn't come naturally to me — something my 4th line Profile and Identity Center to the Throat Center connection likes to avoid at all costs.

Coming out of high school, I knew I wanted to work in the healthcare system and being a doctor seemed like the most "successful" option so it was the first thing I considered. But the part of me that has deep inner knowing that doesn't always make logical sense — the Gates and Channels of the Gnostic circuit — knew that it wasn't the right fit for me. After a couple of years volunteering in various healthcare fields, I landed on physical therapy as my course of study.

As I reflect on this, I see how my logical mind rationalized this decision because I didn't want to repeat the patterns I observed in the parents' of some of my best friends. They weren't around for all our school events the way my parents were and I decided that if I had kids I didn't want to miss out. Turns out I don't plan to have kids, but I didn't know that at the time.

The other thing that drew me to physical therapy vs. becoming a doctor was the deep connection I would build with my patients. I saw the way the healthcare system was changing in the mid-late 1990s and doctors weren't spending as much time with their patients. But as a PT, I saw my patients for up to three hours per week for a month or more. I got to know them on a very deep level, which fulfilled the need for a deep connection of the 4th line in my Profile.

Through these deep relationships with my patients, I started to see how other areas of my patients' lives were impacting the pain that brought them into my clinic. I could see how the stresses of their relationships or their work translated into tension in their necks, shoulders, and backs — how the stresses that they managed through exercises piled up when an injury meant they couldn't run temporarily — and how the things they were eating influenced the inflammation in their bodies, impacting the pain they were experiencing.

And through all of this, I had this feeling that it was important to build a holistic approach. Where many of my colleagues advocated sticking to one modality at a time so that we could know what was working and what wasn't, part of me knew that it was more important to use whatever modalities would get the patient the best results. I was always referring people to massage therapists, acupuncturists, yoga instructors, etc. Collecting resources so that I can feel safe with change is another aspect of my 4th line Profile. And sharing these resources with patients was one of the ways that Integrity — part of my spiritual purpose with Neptune in Gate 26 — showed through me. Another way I stayed in integrity was refusing to see more patients than I felt was appropriate and allowing me to provide great care despite pressure from many bosses over the years as reimbursement took more and more control over care.

This holistic approach became really clear to me when I went through my health crisis. In 2011, while building a referral relationship with an acupuncturist, I decided to try it myself so I knew what I was recommending to my patients. I didn't have any specific issues at the time of my visit, but I had mentioned to him that I'd been experiencing sinus headaches consistently and I'd missed nine days of work that year for abdominal pain. I'd also recently learned that the first PT clinic I'd ever worked in was being gutted due to black mold. He referred me to an environmental medicine physician and it was the first time I'd gotten answers that didn't involve a doctor telling me to just keep taking over-the-counter medications forever.

The treatment for my mold toxicity involved a variety of functional lab tests, the discovery of food allergies that were contributing to my fatigue — which I'd thought was just part of "adulting" because I'd never known a time when I didn't crash on the couch after work and not get up again until bedtime — saunas, yoga, supplements to support my immune system, and more. It was amazing to me that my energy levels could increase so dramatically so quickly with just a few changes. This was the moment I realized I wanted to do more to help my patients move beyond injury recovery and start thriving in their health and wellness.

When I moved back to my hometown in 2012, I was excited to join a team that was innovating the healthcare system by introducing PT-driven wellness. I loved the idea of supporting patients more holistically. But I knew for me to be in integrity, I'd need to level up my skills. I knew that I was strong in the injury recovery and fitness pieces of the puzzle, but for me to help my clients make lasting changes, I needed to learn more about nutrition, behavior change and the psychological aspects that allow people to maintain the lifestyle changes required to have an impact.

When I didn't get the support and guidance I thought was required from management, I went out on my own to further my education through an Integrative Health Coaching Certification through the Institute for Integrative Nutrition. I learned so much about bio-individuality — how what works for one person doesn't necessarily work for the next — meeting people where they are, and helping people come to their realizations about what is the next right step for them. Knowing Human Design would have made this part so much easier as I would have known how to help clients tap into their Truth and next right steps with more confidence!

And as I got further and further into health coaching, I was feeling the pull to move away from physical therapy and went to my boss asking to move more into a coaching role. I loved my patients and the work I was doing with them, but the amount of paperwork and the number of patients I had to see because of the extremely low reimbursement rates in New York was exhausting and completely wore me out. I have a defined Will Center, which means I have the willpower to push through for a while, but this can also be a direct path to burnout if I don't also allow for sufficient restoration to rebuild my resources, including my energy. By the end of the conversation, I thought my boss and I were on the same page when he asked if I would consider coaching through the organization because he didn't want to lose me in the clinic.

So a month later, on September 4 2015, when I was called into his office, I didn't think much of it. We'd regularly have impromptu meetings to talk about marketing, new program ideas, and more. What I wasn't expecting..."You're fired." Maybe not in those exact words, but that was the jist of it.

At first, this shook my identity to the core. Remember...I'd built my whole identity around achievement and being a damn great physical therapist. That's what I thought made me successful and gave me value. But part of me also knew this shakeup was the best thing for me because I was working in a toxic environment and this was the push I needed down a path that required me to reevaluate my career.

I wish this was the point where I say I "woke up" and let go of the beliefs and roles I'd taken on that were keeping me stuck, but this was just the beginning of my self-exploration. Part of me knew this job wasn't the right fit because the implementation of the PT-driven wellness didn't feel good, but I now know that I also have an undefined Spleen Center. This leads me to hold onto things for longer than is good for me so that I feel safe. And the income this job provided allowed me a level of safety and comfort. I immediately replaced this job with another part-time physical therapy job.

About six months before I was fired, I'd started listening to and reading personal development books and podcasts when I started working with a network marketing company in the wellness industry. I wasn't necessarily implementing a lot of the business strategies, but I could feel my mindset shifting. And I loved all the personality assessments that provided insight into who I was and how I worked. While aspects of them felt true, I'd noticed some of them changed from time to time and I always questioned if I was answering them the way I was or how I thought I should be.

The real shift started as my development path took a more spiritual turn. After listening to a podcast, I bolted upright at three o'clock one morning and knew immediately I had to explore tarot cards. With my phone in my hand, hiding beneath the covers so I wouldn't wake my husband, I signed up for some free training through Biddy Tarot and ordered my first deck, the Radiant Rider Waite Tarot deck. I was drawn to Brigit's teachings about tuning into intuition and reading the story in the cards even though I struggled for a long time to let go of the guidebooks. There was something about intuition that felt right to me. (Pluto in Gate 57 — the most intuitive gate in the BodyGraph)

I started attending workshops at a local store, Her Sanctuary, and connected with an amazing spiritual mentor, Punya. I dove into astrology, moon cycles, and meditation with her. I started listening more to my intuition. One of the most profound memories I have came as I was walking into my first moon ceremony. I remember hearing "Just be present and trust the process." It turned out we were doing movement that while somewhat guided involved closing our eyes and listening to what our bodies wanted that evening. I love to dance, but I am the person either on stage performing something choreographed or in the middle of a circle at a party. There is no way you will ever find me dancing on the edges of a circle. But at that moment, I was "dancing" in a storefront window on a busy street where anyone walking by could look in and see. My intuition had told me to be in the moment and trust the process. So I did and it was so powerful. Through my growing relationship with Punya, I was able to release some of the shame and guilt I'd been holding onto for a long time! Thank you Gate 27 — Gate of Accountability in QHD™.

In 2017, I heard a podcast about Human Design and it made a lot of sense to me. I'd learned that I am a Manifesting Generator — Time Bender in Quantum Human Design™. I've started a million things in my lifetime. When something gets me excited I dive all in, but I don't necessarily stick with it until completion or mastery. In college, I minored in Spanish and got really into salsa dancing. A few years later, I bought a digital SLR camera and signed up for a photography course I never finished. I got into scrapbooking after our trip to Australia, but never finished it. My parents would always joke about how I'd get obsessed when something caught my attention — Sun in Gate 29 (Gate of Devotion in QHD™) and Earth in Gate 30 (Gate of Passion in QHD™).

Over time, Greg and I started releasing more of the social pressures in our personal lives to align our lives with what we wanted. We'd decided long ago that we weren't going to have kids. We love the relationships we have with our nieces and nephews, but it didn't make sense for us to have our own. We also realized we were living someone else's dream with a large house and property on the Niagara River that was starting to feel more like a burden on our lifestyle and finances. So when Greg was offered a job that required up to 100% travel in 2018, we knew it was the sign we were waiting for to sell our "dream home" so we could spend more time traveling.

And while I was feeling drawn to all things spiritual and starting to trust myself in my personal life, I was still trying to force my business into the box of clinical health coaching. I took more certification courses to learn to interpret functional lab tests because it felt like the next thing I "should" do. I felt I needed to stay in holistic pain care because I could see a need for it in the world and it made sense with where I'd come from in my career. But something about it didn't feel right. No matter how many marketing courses I took and how many strategies I'd tried to implement, my business wasn't growing because I wasn't fully invested in it.

The pause that came with the pandemic in early 2020 was exactly what I needed to slow down and listen to and reconnect with myself. It gave me something to respond to that made letting go of my health coaching business okay. I had time to reconnect with Punya to play with flower essences and journaling to heal some of the stories and limiting beliefs I'd been carrying and what I thought they meant about me.

I'd known about Human Design for a while, but it came back into my awareness and I realized I wasn't embodying my design. I got support from a coach, Kerri Van Kirk, as I started to explore and play with it in my day-to-day life. I started making small decisions in alignment with my Strategy and Authority — responding to things outside myself and then giving myself time to make sure my sacral response stayed the same. As I got more familiar with what a "yes" and "no" felt like in my body, I was able to apply it to bigger things, starting with what courses to take and what direction my business would go in. And I felt that "hell yes" devotion that told me Quantum Human Design with Karen Curry Parker was something I wanted to dig deeper into.

This playful curiosity I started to approach Human Design with allowed me to lean into the things I'd always felt about myself but had judged because they didn't align with who society told me to be. I started following my "hell yes" and holding the boundaries of my "no." I wasn't perfect, but I started to see my purpose and my dreams more clearly while also learning to let go of fighting for my limitations.

Through the pandemic, Greg and I were living with my parents and nieces and my gram was also part of our quarantine bubble, having dinner with us most nights. I was starting to more accurately interpret the anger and frustration I was feeling as a need for more alone time. It wasn't anything personal toward my family. With an awareness of the needs of the 2nd line in our Profiles and the Gate 40 — Gate of Restoration in QHD™ — in both of our designs, we were able to honor that need for alone time for both of us by going to an Airbnb when we needed a little more space.

That time and space always allowed for the integration that moved me toward the next right steps in my business. I know my work now aligns with my purpose because it feels easier. I have more trust that by connecting to my sacral response, I'm being guided to the next "right" thing, even when it's hard. The "hell yes" I felt for Quantum Human Design™ hasn't dimmed. I get excited about all the ways I can help others embody their Human Design and the Universe keeps bringing me people and things to respond to — Time Bender Strategy.

The way I see it, physical therapy helped me deeply understand the human body while addressing the physical manifestations of stress and burnout. Quantum Human Design™ and the Quantum Alignment System allow me to guide my clients to better understand themselves and their energy so they can prevent burnout or find a more sustainable way back from it. The embodiment piece is the thread that connects the two.

And through the lens of my Quantum Human Design™, I powerfully and passionately declare that my life purpose is to be devoted to showing the world what's possible when we commit to the "right" things, to pushing the edges of authentic self-expression and to inspiring others to do the same by understanding and aligning with their energetic blueprints. I connect to this personal mission statement everyday so I don't lose myself in the expectations of other people or society again and I invite you to connect with your authentic self too so you can let go of the "shoulds" and stand in your power and purpose.

Quantum Human Design™ language © Karen Curry Parker

KRISTEN TOSCANO

~

Kristen Toscano is a physical therapist-turned-Human Design Coach who helps people have more fun, stop taking sh*t from everyone else and become their own authorities. She's been featured on the Understanding Human Design podcast as well as the Quantum Living® podcast where she talks about finding passion and play, learning how to build trust in yourself and your decisions, and creating the life and business of your dreams without burning out in the process. With deep family connections in Buffalo, NY and Boston, MA, Kristen can most often be found traveling the US with her husband Greg.

- You can learn more about Kristen by visiting her website https://kristentoscano.com
- Connect on LinkedIn @kristentoscano
- on Instagram @kristentoscano
- and on Facebook at @lifebyyourdesign

7

A BATH TUB
TRICIA MENDES

Storms

I want you to just hold my hand for a bit.......it will get dark. Just let your heart light the way. My intention is to give you hope, especially if you find yourself in a major life storm that cracks you wide open. Whatever that might be for you. 'Hope' to discover the truth of who you really are. Come with me as I find the real ME and in this deeply vulnerable place, I hope sharing my story helps you on the path to truly finding you. Not the constructed you. The real you. At your very core, your heart, and soul. The you that sometimes needs a storm...

The Break Down Begins

Wednesday, April 11, 2018. I am mentally, spiritually and physically deeply ill. I remember being laid up on the couch with my young daughters at a holiday rental on school break, unable to move. I was burning up, I have never felt anything like it - shards of emotional glass had lodged deeply in my throat. Just to swallow was agonizing. I had plenty to say, but I had buried the words along with my feelings into a dark recess and left them there, discarded. My mind was broken, my heart slammed shut. My soul had escaped into a corner to observe the sorry mess, loath to admit I had utterly abandoned myself.

The old me was breaking down like those shards of glass. I was emotionally and physically bleeding energy. I don't know how I drove us home the next day, but I did.

Fully Cracked Open

9:15 a.m, Wednesday 18th April 2018. My thoughts are in a fully charged blender, relentless, angry, and shouting at me. Guilt, shame, rejection, and the deep unresolved grief from the end of my marriage two years earlier like an iceberg, sat mountainous and undiscovered beneath the surface of my being. The numbness was wearing off and I was assaulted with reality, I could no longer hide the truth to avoid the pain of my past. The darkness needed to come into the light, the pain is excruciating and I can no longer function.

A nagging voice keeps telling me 'You're broken'!

I fill the bath with warm water. Phone softly playing music. I'm so terrified. What is happening to me?

But there is no comfort here. I feel overwhelming hopelessness wash over me like the water. Another voice rises loud above the cacophony in my head. 'Just get it over with, you don't deserve to be here' it spits.

I submit to the voice and begin to fill the bath up further. Slipping into the warm water on a not so average Wednesday morning, my broken heart sits in disagreement. Haven't you forgotten something it asks? I remember my girls.......and in a moment I feel a distinct split in my being. I don't want to live, and I can't leave my girls.

I start to scream.

My soul observing in the corner slams back into my body to lead the charge. I begin pleading for my life from the depths of my core. My intense screams shift dense energy to find the hidden words and I send a prayer loudly out into the invisible realms pleading for help.

Tears stream down my face towards the water that threatens to envelop me as I sob for my life. 'Please, I can't do this anymore, give me a sign that I deserve to get out of this water'. I don't even know who I am talking to. God?

When I reflect on that moment now, there are sounds associated with it. Loud sirens, bells, red flashing lights! Emergency! Emergency! Is there anyone out there listening to me? HELP!

My throat is raw from the screaming, but I NEED to be heard. I'm fighting for my life- I stop for a second to gift myself breath. But what I don't expect is that something would answer me.

It comes seconds after my plea, in the form of a simple text message. In a way that I could not ignore or brush off as coincidence. From an acquaintance that I never expected to hear from. I was offered something almost too good to be true. Miraculous! Something I had wanted to do for a long time. This gift was incredibly generous, and I messaged back to ask why, and could I offer to pay? The response was....'No. It's a gift. You deserve something good to happen today!'

Message received - I get out of the water.

I didn't realize it at the time......but at 9.45 a.m. on a not so average Wednesday morning, I had my spiritual awakening in a bathtub.

The Unknown becomes Known

On some level the deal had been sealed, a clear message delivered from the realms. My soul, like a seed buried into the earth, began to emerge from the darkness. It somehow knows the way.

But there is no compass, no brochure welcoming me, no gold star. Just this incredibly deep sense that something within me had forever shifted. However, I still had this deeply unresolved emotional trauma stored in my mind and body and it needed to be released.

BUT now I know something wants me to BE here.

It becomes my absolute intention to find out why. But first to heal. I didn't know it then, but I had taken a tentative step towards a path of discovery to the most important thing I would ever find - the real Me.

A Thousand Dark Nights

Over the coming years, my depression was devastatingly relentless. I had experienced bouts in the past, but this was different. The energy it took to be in a 'state' of despair and hopelessness for months at a time took a toll on every aspect of my life. My glass was empty - how I chose to fill it was to 'avoid' and numb my feelings with endless window shopping, casual affairs, sleeping tablets, alcohol, and obsessive hours of exercise to obtain the perfect body.

Numbing soon became a significant warning sign for me. My brain would go 'offline.' I can remember several occasions feeling an almost distinct snap from reality. My ability to cope with negative emotions stemming from difficult circumstances was completely zero. My psychological skin was burned and suicidality thinking darkened my days. I recognized none of my old personality traits, my ability to laugh and believe good things happen.

I clearly remember one day at work catching myself laughing at something funny a colleague said. A voice I have come to recognize as my ego quickly admonished me. 'YOU have nothing to laugh about'.

It was a pivotal moment......I had caught the voice red-handed. I couldn't give myself permission to see humor? It was something I truly valued. I was KNOWN as being the Queen of humor! I had cut off from something that made me, me. Laughter was important. What else had I cut off from? The curiosity began to get the better of me. I had to understand my mind.

Ask a Different Question

When you start to ask different questions, you get different answers. It was this curiosity that landed me one Saturday morning in October of 2018 at a free event run by The Life Coaching College in my home city of Melbourne.

Listening to the speaker I was intrigued by her language. What was 'above the line thinking?' and putting yourself into a 'moving towards' state? I felt so aligned with the principals that she was describing. But there was a financial commitment that came with this study. With my spiraling depression and inability to move forward, I had to ask another question. What was the cost of not making the investment? I quickly signed on the dotted line.

Growing Pains

You cannot grow in a different direction in life without feeling discomfort. For something new to come in you must give up something old that is no longer serving you. It requires an up-level in your belief system to recognize where you are creating suffering to allow change. This IS growth.

There were days in the classroom I was immensely triggered. The spotlight was shining in the dark recesses of my mind, showing me the 'broken bits'. There were times I barely held myself together, I felt like an imposter. I continued to persist through the discomfort and discovered my study was life-changing. I now had new knowledge, an ability to see life from a different perspective and a better understanding of how the mind works.

But what no one could teach me, what I failed to understand, and what I still hadn't learned for myself was simply this. The psychological 'armor' that determines how we get through our challenges, my self-love and compassion was still missing in action, I had to re-discover this love and compassion for the me that was desperately trying to emerge from the shadows. I had to find my 'worthiness', my 'enoughness' and allow myself to acknowledge, meet and heal the grief and guilt from my marriage breakdown.

My first suicide attempt went completely unchecked in 2016, it was nearly my last. I believe now I came close to losing my life. I quickly shoved that experience down to sit along with the shame that would not name itself.

I made two other attempts between 2019 and 2020, both times overdosing on sleeping tablets and high levels of alcohol. It was my eldest daughter that found me unconscious one night and called an ambulance. I remember waking up feeling like I was in a vacuum. Where was I? Someone was talking to me as I lay in a hospital bed, but I can't understand the words? Next morning, I put on my clothes and walk out the door without being discharged. No one stops me and no one checks on me. It was like I didn't exist. I walk home from the hospital still substance-affected completely alone. The brutal truth of what had just transpired was yet to hit me.

It was facing the music in the form of my then 15-year-old daughter that slapped me awake. She knew what I had done. She was furious with me. Her furiousness quickly turned to devastating despair when she asked me 'Mum am I not enough?' My shame was unbearable. I made her a promise I didn't know if I could keep, as much as I wanted it to be true. I would never attempt to take my life again. I have kept that promise to this day.

Calling in the Light

I remember one evening in 2017 lying in bed feeling a rare moment of peace. I closed my eyes to rest when an intense explosion of white light filled my eyes. The force of the light was so strong it propelled me into a sitting position and almost jolted me completely out of the bed. The light-filled my room and me and lasted for around three seconds. It was pure love. My Angels had introduced themselves!

I would lay awake at night during my darkest hours and speak to them. Tell them everything.

Through another particularly difficult period, I began to feel the physical symptoms of my emotional pain. In a deeply depressing state one night I felt something I have never felt before. A tar-black, thick crawling energy moving through my torso. I was being consumed with my depressive thoughts manifesting into physical form. These thoughts and actions around death were becoming my reality.

In quick succession, my mother was hospitalized, I had a house fire, another failed attempt at making a romantic connection, and a breast cancer scare. I slept for a month on my living room floor on a single mattress as the fire had damaged my bedroom. I knew on some level that I was receiving warnings. My deceased father came through very strongly around this time and a healer I was working with told me he wanted to 'shake me awake'. For the life of me, I could not find my compass.

So, I began to invite my Angels in on a nightly basis to look over me. I would regularly be rewarded with intense explosions of light. One night I caught a bright glow out of the corner of my eye. I sat up and in the corner of my room what looked like a strobe disco ball was going off with over-head explosions of light! I was literally on the floor hunting for the source only to discover my mobile phone was in a drawer on the opposite side of the room!

My Angels regularly brightened my darkest nights with their light. These encounters filled me with healing. I am so grateful for these heavenly beings taking care of me when I could not take care of myself.

Lessons Learned

I have come to learn that a Spiritual Awakening is not necessarily a conscious decision. Our souls will shift us when we need to grow. For me, it was a major life transition that propelled me into consciousness. But in order to expand, there can be much resistance to letting go. An ability to move forward and let go is a life lesson and it can start with a simple intention.

When we set powerful intentions, a funny thing happens. Life will begin to present us with opportunities to grow toward them and our teachers will appear. It's our job to notice them!

I found myself working with a gifted kinesiologist one day, who identified the deep emotional trauma of my marriage ending. It was so deeply buried it had 'compacted'. Doing this work quickly shifted the stale energy with my husband. We began to move on organizing our financial and divorce settlements after three years.

I also became interested in the art of EFT tapping, or the Emotional Freedom Technique. Searching for a particular tapping script on Youtube one day I came across the work of an incredible physician and intuitive healer that allowed the next level of my healing to occur. I discovered a piece of the puzzle I had been completely missing! I was not allowing myself to meet my heavy emotions with love and compassion. I was doing it blindly with self loathing and frustration. To release these heavy emotions, I had to kindly embrace the lessons they were trying to teach me and allow them to come up safely with love.

Love Yourself

Attending a personal coaching session one day my intuitive coach asked me, 'what happened when you were three?' As a three-year-old child I had a near death experience in a hospital after a procedure and almost bled to death, my mother waiting for me was left in the dark about what was happening and I woke up terrified and alone. This no doubt resulted in trauma and I struggled in the formative years of my childhood, labelled as 'naughty'.

My scared inner three-year-old was screaming at me for attention.

This sense of abandonment was keeping me stuck in a depression cycle I could not escape. I needed to acknowledge my inner child.

I began treating myself like that frightened three-year-old. I finally gave her love and attention. I allowed her to be depressed and sad and fearful. I touched her hair and her face and lovingly told her that she was safe, even with these feelings. I regularly gave her permission to just go to bed and pull up the covers.

I was so exhausted from fighting, so over rejecting the broken parts of me. Done with the suffering that was killing me.

So, I began to LOVE myself back to life.

I have come to learn that self-love is the most precious gift you can give yourself. It is like a shield that protects and connects us to our most divine self. It creates resilience and allows us to move through and with our emotions, not bury them. Self-love is focusing on lessons and growth and holding yourself tight while you do, treating yourself lovingly like a child.

Synchronicity

At the beginning of 2021 as part of my healing, I discovered heart coherence breathing techniques. I became fascinated with the science and realized whilst I knew a lot about the mind, I had little understanding of the power of the heart. I wanted to learn more. As life has it the teacher appeared, I have been diligently working in my heart space healing the cracks with gold. 'Kintsugi'. The Japanese art of repairing broken pottery by filling the cracks with gold. We can absolutely be beautiful again.

Empowered

I like to think that I am my own leader. My own CEO and Coach. My company is ME. Not for monetary profit, my currency is hope. My business is being deeply connected to myself. By virtue of some unseen energy, my healing begins to heal others. Broken things begin to repair, new opportunities present themselves that I never thought possible. Like writing a chapter for this book when I thought my story was over!

I have even found romantic love again. I cannot express my levels of gratitude and appreciation to be able to grow in this space again.

Am I fixed? Do I have it all figured out?

Honestly, my mind is not quite the same. Being in business with myself is a daily investment. I just show up to ME.

My Hope

If this writing touches one person enough to save a life, my work here is done. Globally more than 700,000 people will successfully commit suicide every year. They will never get to share their healing story or give someone else hope to keep going and striving for their authentic truth. I want to open a conversation that allows people struggling with awakening symptoms to openly talk about spirituality and mental health.

Ironically as I write this final piece, the light of the setting sun is streaming through my bedroom window.

So, I will LET IT IN.

TRICIA MENDES

~

How do you find yourself again amidst a catastrophic and life-threatening storm? This empowered question became the catalyst for a path of discovery of the 'authentic' self for this Australian suburban Mother of two. A self that lay so deeply buried under acquired emotional grime in the form of guilt, shame, betrayal, rejection and complete self-abandonment.

'Empowering the self to ask a different question of life can propel us forward into giving ourselves the greatest gift of all. Understanding who we really are at our core in the darkness and in the light'

It was the gift of deep and radical self-love and forgiveness during a life shattering spiritual awakening and bouts of suicidal thinking and behavior, that Tricia transformed years of dark depression, and awoke to become her own New Thought Coach, CEO and Advocate for a conscious and purposeful life.

Follow Tricia on Instagram @trishyeliseawakened

8

KEEP GOING
CHRISTINE GLASNER

They say whatever doesn't kill you makes you stronger. Well, I just turned 53 and while I have not had the hardest life, I have come to believe that what makes us strong is just not giving up. We all have dreams and as life goes on those dreams often change. That doesn't necessarily mean we have given up on our dreams. It just means that as we grow as individuals, our experiences shape us in ways we may have never thought of previously and our perspectives on life and what is important to us also tend to change.

As a teenager in high school, I had the world ahead of me. I was an honor student and had a dream of going into space on the space shuttle. I had been accepted to the University of Alabama in Huntsville, which had a great co-op program with NASA. My high school boyfriend was about to enter the military and I was going to college. We had planned on getting engaged that Christmas and then married when he got out of the service in two years. Shortly after graduation we found out I was pregnant. I was terrified to tell me parents, of disappointing them. I was afraid that all my plans for the future would never come true. We got married seven days later and two days after that he went to basic training. This was deciding moment for me. I could've given up my goals of going to college, but I went to UAH anyway. Well, I went for a semester.

During that semester, the military base doctor said he would not see me if I couldn't promise to have the baby there. I couldn't. So back home I went where I knew my own doctor would see me and I transferred to the local community college to continue my education.

At a doctor's appointment, they did a non-stress test. The doctor didn't like the result and after leaving my mother and I in the exam room for a while, he came back in and instructed us to go across the street to the hospital and that they were expecting us. Inducing labor was not going well and they decided to do an emergency C-section. My daughter nearly died that night. My parents later described what they saw as a scene from a movie. The doors to operating room area burst open as they rushed my baby down the hall to get her to an incubator while they waited for transport to arrive from All Children's Hospital over an hour away.

She was in All Children's Hospital her first two month of life. We lived at a nearby Ronald McDonald House for a month straight and then on and off the next month. Thankfully she survived and after my husband finished his enlistment, we moved back to our hometown. We both got jobs and those initial dreams of flying in space made way for more practical concerns. I'm not sure what made me do it, but one day while I was out, I just stopped in at the community college and signed up for classes. I didn't talk to anyone beforehand about it, I just did it. I finished my A.S. degree and then went on to get a B.S. in Math Education. I know I am a nerd; Math was always my favorite subject in school.

It would be nice to say, 'and they lived happily ever after'. No such luck. Right after my daughter's 14th birthday, my husband announces that he is leaving me. It was such a gut punch. I was not expecting it although on hindsight I guess I should have. He left me for another woman he met online. I thought I was a failure. I would leave school during my planning period and park in an empty church parking lot and cry. I would ask why this was happening to me? What had I done wrong? Why wasn't I good enough? It was a very difficult time for me, always having to appear fine while inside just being torn apart. I not only had to be strong for myself, but for my daughter as well.

Our apartment lease was ending soon, and we had already told the apartment complex that we would not be renewing. We had just put down one thousand dollars to build what I thought was going to be our dream house. I had to go back to the builders and lie about my husband getting a job transfer in order to get our money back. I felt awful about the whole thing. But I was still needing a new place to live for me and my daughter. I suppose I could've gone back to live with my parents for a while or get another apartment, but I didn't. Instead, I went house hunting and bought my first house ever, on my own. The day we closed, my daughter and I brought the tv, blankets and pillows. We ordered pizza and camped out in the living room. That is a moment I will always treasure but moving forward was still very difficult.

I will never forget the turning point for me. A woman who I had certainly not considered a friend at the time invited me out to lunch. I went. She made a comment to me that changed everything. She said, "Don't you realize that you are successful in spite of him, not because of him?" It was like a huge weight had been lifted off my heart. I left that lunch feeling better than I had in months. It was during this time that I found a group of people and started learning about making things happen through intention and found out about the Law of Attraction.

After my daughter graduated, I felt like I needed a fresh start. I moved to another state, got a new teaching job, and bought a house. A couple of years later, I tried leaving teaching and do something new. Out of about 1500 initial applicants nationwide for a training company, I was 1 of 6 that made the cut and the only woman. I was thrilled and loving my new job. But it was not to last. A couple of months in, the company owner's wife was diagnosed with cancer. The owner decided to sell the company back to his former business partner. This is when the proverbial shit hit the fan. The new owner violated our contracts. Nasty emails went flying, threats of lawsuits ensued. It soon became a hostile work environment and I decided I would have to go back to teaching. This was my second attempt at leaving the teaching profession and the second time I had to go back. My self-confidence was suffering, and the following months did nothing to help the situation.

This is now the time of big budget cuts to education and for the first time in my life, I find myself having to accept unemployment. It took me months to find a teaching position. However, that position was only temporary, and it took several more months after that to find the next one. Again, it was temporary. During this time, I often didn't think I would be able to pay my bills. I tried applying for jobs outside of education. For lower paying jobs, I kept being told that I was overqualified because I had a four-year degree. When I tried applying for jobs in the business arena, I couldn't even get an interview because my degree was not business related. I felt stuck. I decided to go back to school. I took out student loans and got my master's degree in business.

It was also during this time that I was getting tired of being alone. Year after year watching those movies on the Hallmark channel and hoping to find someone special. I decided to make a list of the attributes of what I wanted in a partner. I made room in a dresser and in the closet for another's clothes. I was putting into practice many of the things I had learned from a variety of sources but is most easily known as the law of attraction. However, I was impatient and married a man that while not a bad man, was not someone I should have been with. I let my loneliness overshadow the obvious signs. He is an alcoholic and along with is ADHD would result in major mood swings. He would lose his temper and damage things. He would get drunk pretty much every day and if already in a bad mood would wander off. I would not know where he went or what he was doing or when he would be back. His youngest daughter lived with us, and I found myself making excuses for him on a regular basis.

My best friend from college also had a drinking problem. When she died, I went to her funeral. Her husband was very glad to see me, and we talked about what their life had been like in those last few years. I returned home and told my husband that I was not going to live like that. I could not sit back and slowly watch him kill himself. My grandfather had also been an alcoholic and my grandmother had made me promise not to be like her, an enabler. This, he already knew. He knew I did not like him drinking so much. He kept making promises of cutting back and quitting. He would quit, for a while, it never lasted long.

He would be good about it for a couple of weeks, maybe even a month, and then he would decide to take a drink 'to see what would happen'. Or there would be some event that come along that made it acceptable for him, to not just drink but get drunk again. He had even asked me 3 times over the last couple of years if had I wanted a divorce. Each time I said 'no'. In part, I still had this delusion that he would change, and I also knew that if I left, his youngest daughter that lived with us would not graduate high school. So, I stayed.

During our marriage, we acquired several rental properties. I thought we were going to have a business we could do together in real estate. We had eight rental units and I wanted to flip a property. However, in the process of fixing up the rentals we had, it became evident that he did not have the personality to work on the properties. If things did not go right, he would get angry, curse a blue streak, throw and break things. He scared off others that I had gotten to help work on the properties and I got to a point where I told him I would just hire help from then on.

One of the properties we had I had owned before we married. It was empty when the pandemic hit, and I had already started fixing it up to sell. This was also his daughter's senior year of high school. Things were not getting any better for us. I was getting increasingly depressed about my situation. Another friend helped me sort through my feelings. I did a lot of self-reflection and faced realities that I had been refusing to acknowledge. I also realized that one of my biggest issues is not communicating what I want as well as not asking for help. I have been afraid to tell others how I feel and share things openly for fear of what they may think. I have this unrealistic idea that I always need to have things under control, all going to plan, that I can handle anything and everything on my own.

As hard as it was, I left my 2nd husband the summer after the pandemic hit and moved into the house I was renovating. We split the rental properties between us. I had been wanting to start flipping houses for a while, but he did not want to do this. Now that I was on my own again, I started putting things in place to make this happen. I thought I was finally going to start doing something just for me, what I wanted to do. Just over a month later I got a call from my mother. Dad had passed away unexpectedly. My daughter and I went down the next day to be with mom and my sister flew in as well. My sister and I took turns every 2 weeks going to take care of mom because she has dementia. After a few months, this was becoming too much. I sold the house I was living in, put my things in storage and moved in with mom.

I was able to teach remotely that school year, however that was not going to last forever. I sold mom's house and then bought another house back in my state with the help of my realtor and FaceTime. I got a new teaching job, but of course we are back on campus now and I cannot be with mom as much. I have hired someone to come to the house for about two hours a day when I am teaching. She makes mom lunch, takes her for a walk if weather permits and generally keeps here company for a while each day. My grandmother had dementia and now my mom has it. It is highly likely that I will get it. It has been very hard watching her decline over the last year. I know there will come a time when I can no longer care for her in my home as she will need more attention than I can provide. While researching facilities, I have found that it is going to be very costly when mom can no longer stay with me. So now I have put out to the universe my desire to plan for my own future needs and find a way to be home more for mom while she is still able to live with me.

Admittedly, I have not been the best at manifesting intentionally. I have had my greatest successes when what I want is felt and not really thought about. I suppose that is the 'releasing to the universe' part of manifesting. This now brings me to the present. I believe the universe has brought me both of my desires at the same time. I was talking to a friend about needing to plan for future needs when she told me she was working for a company that had a product that she thought was just what I was looking for. I set up an appointment to learn more about it. I was so impressed by it that I joined the company that offers it. In part, due to the pandemic, I will be able to do this job remotely. The company gives me the flexibility to keep my teaching job while I learn about the products and business, and I can switch to full time at my own choosing. So, I will be able to earn money while still being available to my mom. In addition, I will have the opportunity to grow this business in my area and eventually open an office if I chose.

So here I am, the teenage mom with 2 failed marriages, trying to change careers, winding up on unemployment for a time, and taking care of my elderly mother. But this also me, college graduate with an M.B.A degree, real estate investor, teacher, college instructor and entrepreneur. There is no one thing that defines us. Did I have any idea as that teenage mom of all the things that would happen to me to shape my life? No. Do I know what is coming next? No. Will there ever be a 'happily ever after' for me? Who knows? What I do know, is that I will keep going. I don't know how to do anything else. Life is always going to throw those curve balls just when we think we have everything in place. Sometimes those curve balls are opportunities in disguise. Sometimes, they feel like it is the end of the world, and you just don't know how you are going to move on. But it doesn't matter how many times we are knocked down. What matters is that we keep getting back up. I also know that we are all a work in progress. My journey of self-improvement is ongoing, and I look forward to each new stage in my development.

CHRISTINE GLASNER

~

Christine Rabell Glasner is a veteran teacher, experienced corporate trainer, real estate investor, and entrepreneur. Her teaching experience spans from middle school to community college. Her love of real estate began when her only daughter got her hooked on the HGTV show Trading Spaces. This has led to a love of DIY, owning multiple rental properties, and looking forward to her first flip in the near future.

She loves attending the Carolina Renaissance Festival, having a girls' day out with her daughter, and spending time with her grandkids. She is now also taking care of her mother, who has dementia. This has led to her investigating the need to prepare for the future. This search has led her to join Premier Financial Alliance and a goal of spreading the word about living benefits in the hopes that she can help other families prepare for whatever their futures hold.

You can connect with Christine on her Facebook page: https://www.facebook.com/christine.r.glasner
Or on LinkedIn: www.linkedin.com/in/christine-glasner-8205a145

9

STEPPING INTO THE AKASHIC GATEWAY

YUMIE ZEIN

Stepping Into The Akashic Gateway

People often ask what was the single most important event that led to the reset of my entire life. Even though it was a culmination of many events, if I was ever to choose one moment in time after which my life was never the same, it would be when I connected to the Akashic Records, or rather, when they found me.

How beautiful it is to look back and see the trail of breadcrumbs that the Universe had so intelligently placed. I truly believe that there are no accidents, no coincidences, no haphazard situations that you experience, or random people that you meet. Life is a mysterious performance in which you are the music, the maestro, the dancer, and the audience all at the same time. With that belief in mind, a whole new world emerges in front of you, the veils of illusion lift and you remember that you came here to play. To forget that you remember, and then remember that you forgot. Ultimately, you are the Universe understanding itself.

But I get ahead of myself. Let's start at the beginning if there was ever such a thing.

In this lifetime, I chose to come to play as an Egyptian-born woman raised between the Middle East and Egypt in conservative Islamic societies. Growing up, I always felt like I didn't quite fit in anywhere no matter how hard I tried. I was an overweight child and continued to be well into my adolescence. Being in an emotionally unavailable household where physical and verbal abuse was a common occurrence, I found my solace in food and books. I poured myself into any book I could find and from a very early age, possibly around eight or nine, I discovered that it was relatively easy for me to do well in school because of that. From then and up until I graduated high school, I compensated for my lack of social and emotional skills by being the well-known overachiever in every school I went to. My value was solely based on how well I did and how high of a grade I got. I had to be top of the class, any class, otherwise, I felt worthless.

My lack of self-worth was amplified by the fact that I was made to wear the Islamic veil or Hijab as soon as I hit puberty. At the tender age of 12, I still vividly remember the feeling of having to cover up the first time. It felt like some kind of sin to have turned into a woman. There was a deep rage bubbling up inside me that had nowhere to go. That day, I aged a hundred years or more. I cried silent tears in bed and screamed into my pillow. I immediately disconnected from my body. It felt like it was no longer a safe place, that it was the cause of my imprisonment, the loss of my innocence and childhood.

It felt like a curse being a woman. My voice didn't matter, my feelings didn't matter. Those were the rules and I had to comply. That's just the way it was. A solemn heaviness landed in my heart and throat that stayed with me for decades. I hated God — I hated religion. I felt betrayed by the people closest to me. I wanted nothing to do with any of it. I rebelled in any way I could but the more I rebelled the more violent things got. I had very few friends and no one with whom I could actually share any meaningful conversations. I cried myself to sleep many nights. I planned to run away and when it didn't work, I frequently contemplated suicide. It took years but eventually, I got the rebellion beaten out of me. I was numbed out in every way possible and threw myself further into food and academics.

I now know that my family did the best they could with what they knew at the time. Their own trauma, fears, and wounds were the driving force behind their actions. I have so much love and compassion for them. There was a lot of dysfunction and toxicity present on many levels during my childhood and adolescence and no resources or tools to address them. Mental health was and still is, a huge taboo in Arab countries. Nevertheless, I am grateful for the roles my family chose to play. There was never any malicious intent. The experience of having my free will disregarded fueled a passionate desire for the rebellion that I am infinitely grateful for. If it wasn't for that rebel that continued growing inside me ever so silently, I would have continued to force myself into the mold that was expected of me. To me, that would have been the ultimate tragedy.

In the years that followed, I graduated as a chemical engineer and landed a prestigious corporate job in the oil and gas field. By then, I was solely operating from my masculine side. That was the only energy that felt safe. The overachiever inside me was satisfied with graduating from one of the hardest majors in university and entering a purely male-dominated field. On some level, I felt like I was sticking it to the patriarchy, that this was somehow redeeming the sense of shame and guilt that I felt for being a woman. But with that, there came a never-ending checklist that I felt I needed to complete to remain worthy of that redemption. A constant need for validation, applause, approval, or acknowledgment.

Life was good at the surface level but my soul was screaming out in agony. I gained a huge amount of weight and was at my lowest level of self-esteem. I decided to undergo bariatric surgery in my early twenties that almost killed me. Due to developing post-op pneumonia after the surgery, I was placed on a ventilator for about a week. Late one night, the ventilator mysteriously decided to stop functioning. My mother was in the room with me and she started to panic as I began to thrash around in bed. As my ears started ringing, I could hear her voice sounding very far away as she ran out of the room to find a doctor. For about three minutes my airway was completely cut off. The ringing in my ears intensified and my vision was rapidly fading away. Everything suddenly turned white, I stopped thrashing around and a wave of peace overcame me.

"Oh. So this is how I'm going to die.", I thought to myself matter-of-factly. There was no fear, no struggle, just a strange sense of sadness mixed with slight disappointment. At the same time, I heard another voice saying, "But there's still so much to do!". It was at that very moment that a doctor came rushing into the room and restarted the ventilator.

That was my first encounter with the other side. It created a mix of shock, curiosity, and immense gratitude inside me. It felt like a strong message to change directions, to re-examine my life, to slow down. Sadly, I did not heed that message and went right back to my old life once I recovered physically.

But, of course, the messages did not stop —

A few years later, in the early morning hours of Saturday 1/1/11, I was driving to work. It was the first day of the New Year, a public holiday and a weekend yet the overachiever inside me couldn't resist the urge to get some work done. I was on the corporate hamster wheel and unable to get off, or rather, not even aware of its existence. A jaywalker suddenly rushed onto the highway wanting to cross to the other side. As I veered sharply to avoid hitting him, the car started to spin violently and then proceeded to lift off the ground and flip over. I remember watching all of this happen in slow motion. My laptop and other belongings were flying around inside the car as it rolled over not once, not twice, but three times, finally landing on its side. I was suspended in mid-air, held only by my seatbelt, and I remember waiting for the cars driving on the highway to come crashing into me.

"Oh. So this is how I'm going to die.", I thought again to myself matter-of-factly. And once more a wave of peace washed over me, mixed with that familiar sense of sadness and slight disappointment. There was no second voice this time though, instead, I felt a distinct protective presence placing a bubble around me. I knew I wasn't alone. The energy was so strong that I could almost feel it with my hands. I felt safe. I felt loved. I felt supported. A few moments later, a police car came driving by and stopped traffic. They turned my car right side up and were amazed that I came out without a single scratch. That sense of shock, curiosity, and immense gratitude again percolated inside me. I spent some time contemplating the miracles that have saved my life twice so far. There was a slightly deeper awareness of the message being sent. My car symbolized my direction in life and I was being asked to slow down, to stop, and reassess. Once more I did not heed that message. The next day, I took a taxi to work, sore body and all.

But, of course, the messages did not stop —

A couple of years later, as I continued to check off my checklist, I was higher up the corporate ladder, still burning myself out at work, only now I was also married with a one-year-old girl and studying to complete a Masters degree in engineering management. For anyone observing on the outside, it was a picture-perfect life, but in reality, I was dying inside. I had ticked off everything that I thought was going to finally make me feel loved, worthy, successful, and yet there was a gaping void inside of me. It made no sense. One evening as I was getting ready for bed, I felt a sharp stabbing pain on my right side and was rushed to the ER. The doctors told me I had severe kidney inflammation and that my right kidney was functioning at only 10%. I spent some very challenging weeks in the hospital. At some point, there was talk of the need to completely remove my right kidney to avoid further complications. Doctors were clueless as to how this can happen so suddenly. I had never had any kidney issues. That shook me up. My own body was failing me and I was barely 30 years old — Something had to change.

Unbeknownst to me, kidney issues symbolized holding in fear, resentment, and an inability to process intense emotions which was most likely the culmination of the past three decades of my life. In hindsight, this made perfect sense but at the time I was oblivious to it. However, my body forcing me to a complete halt allowed me to deeply re-examine my life. At the time, I was living in Egypt and I came to the realization that I did not desire for my daughter to grow up in the same society that I had experienced. I began to consciously research immigration options and applied to any program I could find — from Australia to New Zealand to Canada to the U.S. I felt like I was being guided by an incessant force that had been unleashed and refused to be ignored any longer. I didn't have a plan and couldn't even formulate one. For once, I allowed myself to be led, to believe in infinite possibility, to trust in the unknown, and let go of expectations.

Months later, I opened my laptop one morning and an email popped up announcing that my application to the U.S Diversity Lottery program was selected. It was another miracle. Out of all the immigration programs I had applied to, this was the only one that relied on a computerized random selection process. Millions of people apply every year and only a minuscule number gets selected. I knew people who had applied for over 10 years in a row without being selected. I had literally won the lottery! It confirmed to me that I was indeed being led. A deeper sense of trust and belief was blossoming inside of me.

Little did I know that this was just the beginning of the journey towards fully surrendering to the Universe. It was the start of letting go of all the checklists I had spent years ticking off. I quit my nine year career, packed up my life, and moved with my then-husband and daughter to Houston without any clue of what was to come. As the external things that I used to identify myself with began to fall away, I fell into the deepest depression I had experienced so far. I felt like a complete failure. I didn't know who I was, what I liked or disliked, what I believed in, what I valued, what I wanted with my life, or why I had made the choices I did. I knew nothing except that I was suddenly drowning in a tsunami of emotions. I hit rock bottom and I now see the immense blessing and wisdom in it. The desperation I was feeling and the sensation that my entire life was crashing down pushed me to explore and wander into areas of myself that I would have never otherwise approached.

I began bingeing on self-development topics, coaching, therapy and anything I could get my hands on that seemed like it would shed some light on what was happening with me. This new world of self-discovery felt entirely foreign to me and I was constantly asking for guidance, clarity, and for support as I began to follow the trail of breadcrumbs.

My research led me down the rabbit hole of energy healing and I "coincidentally" came across a website that mentioned Sekhem healing, an ancient Egyptian energy healing modality. Being Egyptian, this peaked my fascination and I felt drawn to connect to an online transmission that was being offered. I went to sleep later that night, thinking nothing much of it. Early the next morning as I stood alone in the kitchen making breakfast for my daughter, I suddenly heard a massive gong-like sound that reverberated from somewhere above my head and then immediately felt an intense wave of electric-like energy pass through my body from head to toe. I was stunned in place and unable to comprehend what just happened. As I began frantically looking around to see if the sound could have come from any physical object nearby, my eyes fell on two Egyptian statues that I had brought with me from Egypt a year earlier and had casually placed on the countertop directly facing me. They were the statues of Anubis, the symbol for death, and Isis, a representation of rebirth, love, and magic. At that moment, crystal clear clarity dawned upon me. I knew that a gateway had been opened but I had no idea where it would end up leading me.

That experience in the kitchen propelled me much deeper into ancient Egyptian spirituality. It felt like finally coming home. As I was studying material about the Emerald Tablets of Thoth, there was mention of the Halls of Amenti and the Akashic Records. A strange sense of familiarity and remembrance washed over me and I felt an incessant urge to find a mentor to teach me how to connect to these energies. For the next year, I poured myself into learning and connecting with the Records under several mentors and through my own inner explorations.

The journey with the Akashic Records brought me endless opportunities and gifted me with numerous miracles. I became connected to a spiritual plant medicine community that provided me with a sense of family and belonging. I no longer felt alone and misunderstood. After 20 years of wearing the veil, on February 22, 2019, I chose to take it off and it was like a mountain of physical and energetic baggage was lifted off my shoulders. I let go of my marriage, my past career, my religious belief system, and the long list of labels I had used to identify myself. I became nothing and everything.

I was finally free —

It was then that I felt called to support other women through the process that I had gone through. I began to learn how to lead women's circles and through that magical process, I began to heal my wounds related to embracing my femininity, sexuality, and sensuality. I was blessed, and continue to be blessed, with the opportunity to support numerous women through breakthroughs, expansions, and healing journeys and have experienced authentic, loving, powerful sisterhood connections beyond anything I could have ever imagined.

My life has blossomed into a continuous stream of miracles albeit with its continuous stream of lessons and growth opportunities too. The difference now is that I have an intimate relationship with myself and the Universe because I know we are never separate. Looking back on the experiences that shaped my journey so far, I am truly humbled and grateful beyond words. There is a beautiful saying that goes, "Your mess is your message." What seemed like a messy, dark, hopeless journey was the preparation to guide others through a similar path.

We each have a story to tell, and there is a unique power in each one. I hope that sharing my journey may have helped shed some light on the truth of who you are, who you really are. May you always remember.

I am You, You are Me, We are One — We are the music, the maestro, the dancer, and the audience all at the same time.

YUMIE ZEIN

Yumie Zein is an international best-selling co-author of the book —365 days of Self-love—. As an Egyptian Creatrix, Akashic Alchemist, Hypnotist & Sacred Circle Holder, she incorporates ancient wisdom with New Earth teachings to bring about unique transformation and self-empowerment. Her passion and curiosity about the Akashic Records sparked her awakening several years ago leading her into the work she does today. Yumie incorporates transformative spiritual coaching techniques, energetic clearings, deep mindset shifts, and Akashic downloads to assist you in aligning with your highest timeline and uncovering your hidden gifts.

To connect:
Facebook: https://www.facebook.com/Yumie1111
Instagram: @Yumie1111
Youtube: @Yumie Zein
Website: www.OfHeavenOnEarth.Com
Email: Yomna@OfHeavenOnEarth.Com

10

SURVIVING BLUE BIRD ~ A STORY OF COURAGE AND RESILIENCE

ROXY RAPEDIUS

"Some people survive and talk about it. Some people survive and go silent. Some people survive and create." ~ Nikita Gill, "People Survive in Different Ways" - The Minds Journal

My childhood vivid and happy memories started when I was nine months old. I remember being free-spirited, strong-willed, full of life, and marching to the beat of my drum from the get-go and I attribute this tenacity to my parents' loving, supportive, and empowering teachings. I was surrounded by wonderful close-knit siblings, grandparents, aunts, uncles, and cousins. My brother and I are 21 months apart, and my sister is 65 months. A beautiful loving family.

The Year Everything Changed

In second grade, I was chosen by the principal of our school to join a meditation group of about six students where we would meet every morning to meditate. I honestly did not know it was a meditation group until I started meditating as an adult. I firmly believe these meditations helped shape who I am today.

The summer of 1975 changed my life forever. I was a happy eight-year-old girl with great friends having so much fun until trauma hit me. I was sexually abused in the basement of our church by the custodian. Along with the abuse, he threatened to kill my family and tell everyone I was a bad girl. This is when I lost my inner child, my self-confidence, self-esteem, and where all my self-limiting beliefs began. I skipped my childhood and teenage years by taking care of everyone else. I became a super competitive perfectionist which are traits of being sexually abused. I never told a soul as I was so scared of losing my family. As a defense mechanism, I repressed the memories in the deepest recesses of my brain for thirty years.

Less than three years later, I lost one of the most influential people in my life, my paternal grandmother. I shared so much with her. We spent time cooking, baking, playing cards, and watching tv. I would put curlers in her hair and help her do the laundry. She would allow me to put the wet clothes through the wringer before hanging them on the clothesline outside. We were extremely close and I loved her so much. I was devastated, yet kept ongoing. I was going to show the world that I was strong and a good person.

Showing the World I Was a Strong and Good Person

As a child, I played, created, and tried to have fun with my friends. I always excelled in school and extracurricular activities and was often chosen to attend leadership camps from a young age. My outside self-image showed that I was strong and powerful however inside I was screaming and in a lot of turmoil. I never felt that I was good enough, beautiful enough, strong enough. I always tried to do more to ensure I was recognized and appreciated.

I pursued gymnastics and didn't excel at it. It wasn't my favorite sport, however, I kept practicing. Feeling less than, not good enough, a big failure. Bowling was probably my saving grace. Started in a league at a very young age and became very good at the game, winning many competitions and even appeared on TSN Pins Game in my adult years. I was proud of my achievements yet it wasn't good enough, I needed to do more.

Why Couldn't He Just Love Me? The Battle of Self Worth

At the age of 13, I started a relationship with a boy older than me. I felt loved, heard, and appreciated. As the years went by, he started treating me like sloppy seconds, and the love and appreciation slowly dissipated. I vividly remember my mom and aunt telling me he was mistreating me and I didn't believe them. I was afraid of being alone and never finding another boyfriend. The relationship became conditional and every bad thing that happened to him was my fault. We were fighting constantly yet I always wanted to make things better. Hated confrontation and consistently sacrificed myself to make him happy. Resentment set in and my heart was breaking. Hearing through the grapevine that he was sleeping around with other girls was the last straw on the camel's back. I ended the relationship before starting University. Despite the good decision, more feelings of not being enough, being a failure, it's your fault kept on creeping in. What is it that I could have done better? Why couldn't he just love me? I absolutely did everything for him!

Striving, Succeeding, and More Tragedy

I started working at the age of 15 during the summer months in two restaurants during the week and Mike's Milk Convenience Store on weekends. I loved working at all three places as my employers were great. One night, at Mike's Milk, I was held up at gunpoint to empty the cash register. What a crazy scary night. I ended up going to work the next morning. I was actually scared shitless but needed to move on. I needed to show that I was strong, committed and nothing would bring me down.

The first day of grade 10 would be another traumatic day for me. The day I lost my best friend to suicide, the day where I started feeling guilty and blaming myself for his passing. If only I was a better friend and talked to his parents about his feelings, he would still be alive today. I held this guilt and blame for over 22 years and simply swept it under the carpet and continued with my life. Although difficult, I ended up having an amazing time in high school. My friends were wonderful and the teachers were so awesome. I was involved in Band, became the trainer for the Girls' Basketball Competitive Team, and was part of the Prom Organizing Committee. At the end of Grade 11, I was hired to teach in Summer School with one of my teachers. Such a wonderful experience.

During my high school years, I also played baseball in a women's league. Although I was good at it and had fun, the constant inner turmoil was always present. The vicious self-talk continued ... you're not good enough, you can do better, what's wrong with you, you're a failure, you can't meet people's expectations, you're not beautiful, you're fat, etc.....and I became a fixer and stronger perfectionist. Couldn't move on until things were completed and done a certain way. I was helping everyone with their problems yet no one would change or make things better. I forever carried their burdens, their sadness, their grief on my shoulders and kept plowing through. Graduated from university in 1989 with a Bachelor of Arts and started my first full-time job as a word processor for a Trust Company.

Bright Beginnings

I married when I was 23 to an amazing man. Life was great for the first six years of our marriage. We lived in Ottawa, had good jobs, and were amazing friends. One evening while watching a program on TV, I asked my husband if I was his "world." Without a flinch, he responded a flat no! His world was his job! Everything changed that night!

Although I was thriving at work, winning awards, getting promotions, spending time with wonderful friends and family, I felt like a failure. The inner critic was getting louder.

We tried for three years to have a baby with no luck. Three years of abdominal surgeries, pricking and probing, having sex early in the morning, and rushing to the doctors to see if the swimmers were making it to my eggs, taking fertility drugs, gaining tons of weight, and absolutely nothing....my life was shattered...I so wanted to be a mom. I wholeheartedly believed that I would be the "world" to my child and this would fix my marriage. People thought we were the perfect couple. Never fought in public....I pretended to be someone I was not. For the next nine years, I felt less then, not being enough, a failure. Ok....time to fix and help others! Sleeping was becoming a challenge ... .sleepwalking became the norm...off to the sleep clinic I went to and nothing but "you're stressed" came out of it. I needed to decompress and was put on sleeping medication.

I became a big sister and group leader with the Big Sisters of Ottawa-Carleton. My little sister, who was six and a half years old at the time, became my whole world. She brought love, happiness, and joy to my life. Our weekly visits, family dinners, sleepovers and camping weekends gave me purpose and kept me going! She was a fighter and a leader, a mini-me! She was a disco ball in my dark world, the epitome of who I wanted to be. She was bubbly and always striving for excellence, winning online writing contests and graduation principal awards. Creating little jobs and marketing pamphlets to make some money. "I can't" was not part of her vocabulary. Today, at 34 years of age, she is the most beautiful confident person I know. She has two masters, traveled the world, created her own little business, and works for an amazing company. She is an outstanding leader and is surrounded by a plethora of friends and beautiful family. I am blessed to have her in my life!

Sept 11, 2001, was the catalyst to my life-changing. It was the day I decided that I needed to move closer to my family, my support system, my home-town. My husband was transferred in January 2002 and I moved in May. I took a full year off and began working on myself. I completed a course in Interior Design, spent time with my friends, nieces and nephews, and family. In 2003, I started a job in financial planning, bought my very own car, and continued investing in myself by working on my inner self talk, my limiting beliefs, confidence, self-esteem. Although people were telling me I was a wonderful person, caring, giving, kind, etc, and brought so much to their life, I simply didn't believe it. The daily vicious self-talk was telling me otherwise: you are not enough, you are a failure, you can't do anything right, your marriage is failing, you don't have enough money, what is wrong with you...suddenly the anxiety and panic attacks started, I developed a nodule on my thyroid gland, I was no longer healthy....

So, I joined Boards, volunteered, organized a Ladies' Day, joined a bowling and baseball league and Dragon boat team, keeping me so busy that I didn't have to deal with my failing marriage. In early 2004, my husband decided he wanted to change his career from loans manager to truck driver. He hated his current job and wanted to be on the road. Off he went! I believed that this new job would bring us closer and it didn't.

My husband became my roommate. Gone all week and back home for a few hours on the weekend. I never really spent quality time with him as I was busy preparing his meals for the following week and cleaning the house while he sat watching TV to decompress from the week.

Finally Living for Me

Shortly after he started trucking, I started seeing this wonderful medium and life coach. Holy shit on toast, the flood gates opened up. In the first session, the repressed memories of being sexually abused and my friend's suicide came up with a vengeance. I had never cried like that before. Those secrets that I kept locked up all those years burst out of my heart and suddenly allowed me to start healing and grieving. I felt this heavy burden being lifted from my shoulders. That night, I slept like a baby. I learned how to forgive others and myself for what happened all those years ago.

I knew I still had a lot of work to do, however, it provided me with the opportunity to finally grow into the person I wanted to be. For years I looked to people to give me what I needed; happiness, joy, love, advice on decision-making, the justification that I was a beautiful and wonderful person, and validation that I was doing the right thing. I solely relied on what they said about me and viewed the world accordingly. Before the session, I was living my life according to what I felt others wanted me to be. I lived to please others, to stop confrontation and fix everybody's problems, and firmly believed this would bring me everything I needed to live a fulfilled life......WRONG.....all it did was deflate and stress me out because people started expecting me to do everything I did for them all the time. Although successful in many areas of my life, I was still not enough and a failure.

I continued to dig deep into my life to find out where my core beliefs and values came from to define the real me and discover my self-worth. I used to believe that hustle, bustle, and grind was the only way to achieve wealth, abundance, an amazing career, and wonderful life. Boy was I mistaken! Don't get me wrong, is hard work necessary? Hell yes, however, it doesn't have to include burnout, anxiety and fear. And you don't need to be a mom to be BADASS!

In June 2005, after 15 years of marriage, I separated from my husband. Found the courage to do what was needed for me and no one else. Of course, it was a shock to everyone as we were seen as the best couple ever. The advice started pouring in whether I wanted to hear it or not: what will people think, you should try to fix your relationship, he's such a great guy, you must make sacrifices in life, marriage is not always rosy....I heard it all. I stood my ground and plowed through it all. I was no longer listening to people's opinions and advice about my life. Only I could define my worthiness, the woman I wanted to be, and the life I wanted to live. I held my head high, quit my job, and moved to Hamilton in September to start a new life. I found a job, not exactly what I wanted, however, I knew that I would land on my feet and started seeing a wonderful man. I finally believed that I was smart, enough, successful, beautiful, badass and that I could achieve anything I wanted! There was no room for negativity. Once I started living in a positive way, I started to motivate and inspire others without even trying. I no longer sought love or approval, it was coming freely and I felt like a million dollars!

Attracting Love and Abundance

Randy came into my life at the right time, he was a godsend. He continues to inspire, encourage and comfort me. He is supportive in everything I do and makes me smile every day and finds joy in loving me. He fills my heart and soul with laughter and joy. I cherish every moment we share together and find comfort in just sitting with him without words. He makes my soul stronger!

His parents accepted me with open arms as the daughter they never had. With his two beautiful daughters, our relationship flourished and we married in 2010. I was involved in Randy's youngest daughter Marissa's hockey. Became a board member of the hockey association she played for and started playing in a women's hockey league as well. In July of 2012, Amanda, the oldest daughter, and I toured Italy for 14 days. Amanda was able to see places she had studied in some of her history classes. I loved every minute of that trip; I made great memories that I will cherish forever. I love those girls like they were my daughters.

Although Randy and I faced many adversities such as health problems, family issues, the passing of loved ones, loss of jobs due to realignment, we plowed through them together. In 2013, after a routine ablation surgery, I was hospitalized for 11 days with sepsis and acute peritonitis. It was a touch and go situation as my body was shutting down. I remember laying in the hospital bed thinking I can't die; I still have way too much to do and accomplish! I felt deep in my core that my real purpose was not achieved yet. Randy and I started to travel more and enjoy life to the fullest.

In November 2016, after studying for five years part-time while working, I graduated Honors from the Addiction Program at McMaster University. I was so proud to achieve this milestone at the age of 49 and receiving my diploma with my husband, sister, mom, and two amazing friends by my side was just beautiful. I was extremely happy and floating on cloud nine.

Surviving Bluebird

In early 2017, I signed up to volunteer at a grief and bereavement camp for children aged 6-17 through The Bob Kemp Hospice and began my training. There are no words to express the gratitude and love I felt after the training was over. The learnings and appreciation I received through the training was incredible and fully prepared me for the camp weekend. My grief and bereavement weekend at Camp Erin with 49 kids was out of this world. I had such an awesome time. The weekend was filled with singing, playing, talking, swimming, laughing, and crying. It was such an overwhelming experience yet so heartfelt. I never thought that I could spend a full weekend with kids (6 to 14 years of age) dealing with grief and bereavement. I must say that I learned so much from all of them. They were so courageous and honest while telling their stories during the memory wall ceremony. The activities like canoeing, fishing, polar bear dip, rock climbing, painting memory boxes, painting luminary bags, making dream catchers, the drumming circle, the sacred fire, the luminary ceremony, the singing lunches, and egg team building event brought take away learnings to help the kids cope with their grief and daily life. It was astounding to see the positive change the weekend brought on from the time they came on the bus to the time they were dropped off to their parents. Although there were tears and sadness, there was an abundance of joy, bonding, and relationship making. This was an experience of a lifetime!

Following that weekend, I started training for palliative support at the hospice. This beautiful place gives me peace and grounds me. I love spending time helping people transition through their end of life, listening to their stories, or simply holding their hands while they sleep. I take comfort in being there for them.

One of the patients I was supporting called me her bluebird because I brought her joy during her transition period. She said, "Roxy, you have no idea how I love getting together with you. You make me feel safe and at peace. Never change your authenticity for anyone. You are a kind and beautiful soul." She made a huge impact on my life and our short time together propelled me to become a life coach. I became certified in March of 2018 with CCF and with John Maxwell in August 2018. Life coaching has enabled me to help people grow and be the best version of themselves; to achieve anything they want in life; to live in abundance, achieve happiness, freedom, and purpose by surrounding themselves with people that support them, love them, and raise their vibration and have the best relationships ever.

Subsequent to my first certification and logo creation, I was faced with excruciating news on April 11, 2018. I was diagnosed with Cancer - Follicular Lymphoma of the Duodenum. My heart sank....I couldn't believe hearing the words coming out of my doctor's mouth. He provided me with an oncologist referral, said he was really sorry, gave me a big hug, and sent me on my way. I was in shock and cried the whole way home and didn't really know how to tell my husband. During the 10-minute ride home, my mind started making plans for treatment, backup plans in case the treatment didn't work, getting my affairs in order...it was pure hell. When I got home and started telling my husband, I simply lost it. I was drained, with no energy left in my body. That day, I was very adamant with my husband. No one was to know, not even my family or the kids. I wanted to have my appointment with the oncologist to discuss the type of cancer, the treatment, and the next steps. I wanted to be informed prior to the news coming out. Why get everyone worried when I didn't understand it myself? I wanted to have all my shit together then talk.

I waited 3.5 months to see my oncologist....the worst time of my life. I was living on fumes....no energy left and so deflated. In the appointment, I learned that cancer I had was a wait and see cancer. Unless I was in pain or uncomfortable, there really wasn't any treatment for it. I had done a lot of research on my own and felt comfortable with his recommendation - now I could tell my parents and siblings. That day, I decided that this cancer would not win! In late August, an ad for Dr. Joe Dispenza showed up on my FB Feed. I had never heard of him, however, the message on the ad caught my eye -" Becoming Supernatural." Clicked on it and registered for his Progressive and Intensive Online Course. It was amazing! A course to get you out of your comfort zone, push you beyond your limitations, and challenge your very perception of reality. It provides cutting-edge science, inspiring lectures, real-life case studies, and powerful meditation and visualizations. By applying the teachings you can overcome challenges throughout any arena of your life. I learned and applied every lesson. I saw myself living healthy and happy every day of my life. My home was also cleared of all chemicals, toxins, and pollutants. I changed all the cleaners, detergents, soaps, hair products, skin lotions, and make-up to natural and safe products. Through a naturopath, I was able to take a hormonal test, start the Keto lifestyle and readjust all my minerals and supplements enabling me to lose 65 lbs, re-balance my hormones, put my Hashimoto Autoimmune Disease in remission, sleep better, decrease my hot flashes and give me tons of energy! In Feb 2019, I had a GI done and they couldn't see anything in my duodenum. They scheduled a follow-up GI in March of 2020. Due to Covid, it was pushed to Aug 2020. A GI and a biopsy was done and sent to pathology. Received a call from my surgeon saying: I don't know what you are doing, however, keep it up....the cancer is gone and the pathologist and I are extremely happy! Best news received that day!

The bluebird is a symbol of hope, love, and renewal, the essence of life and beauty. It also represents happiness, joy, fulfillment, hope, prosperity, and good luck. I am deeply touched by being called a bluebird because I truly believe that I represent all the above. With courage, resilience, and change in mindset you too can become a <u>**Surviving Blue Bird & Warrior**</u>. Your past traumas and tribulations do not define who you are, YOU, and only you can define the person you are or want to be! Simply make the decision to be the best version of you today!

I healed my inner child, my cancer, and absolutely love the beautiful, successful, and worthy woman I am today. I'm enjoying my career, my business, being a wife, step-mom, daughter, sister, friend, and an OMA to two beautiful grandchildren. I'm powerful and know that I am changing thousands of lives through life coaching.

With gratitude, Roxy xo

ROXY RAPEDIUS

~

Roxy Rapedius is a published author in Brainz Magazine and lives happily with her husband in Hamilton ON Canada. Roxy's decades of professional experience include progressively increasing responsibility and measurable positive results. The significant and unique skills built through these roles have enabled Roxy to easily move to her entrepreneurial role of CEO and Executive Mindset & Wellness Coach where she empowers individuals through change, transition, and transformation.

As CEO and Life Coach With Roxy, she approaches her work and life as an established leader who gets results. Roxy has a plethora of experience across different industries. Her current focus and passion are helping people to realize their spiritual tools to achieve success. Roxy is very passionate and dedicated to enhancing the lives of those she touches by helping them reach their goals. Roxy believes that wellness matters in every aspect of our life: physical health, environmental (including our home, our community, and the world itself), personal/work life, and financial. Roxy has a curiosity and keen desire to always further expand her knowledge and acumen to reach greater heights in serving others as a leader in business and life.

You can visit her online at

- www.wellnesswithroxy.com
- https://linktr.ee/Lifecoachwithroxy

11

SEASONS OF LOVE, LOSS AND PERSONAL POWER

KIM TREMBLAY

I got married at a young age. I was pregnant, 17 years old, turned 18 the next month and had my daughter 2 months later. I was very naive, quite isolated and young for my age. I am the oldest of four children. When I told my parents, (well actually they guessed) I had to stay in my room for what felt like a couple of days. Finally, the father came over to talk to my dad and they were swimming in the pool together. At that time, I was able to come out of my room and I was told "well, you will get married". I honestly did not feel like I had a choice. A wedding was planned real quick and the reception was held in my parents rec. room.

We met in grade 10 and were high school sweethearts. He played on the football team, had access to a car and was so very cute. He was the perfect gentleman, always looking out for me and treating me like gold. He would walk to pick me up, back to his parents house and then walk me home. We had a lot of fun back in those days, smoked a lot of pot and just hung out with friends, mostly his or maybe all his when I think about it.

I remember when I was in high school in my physical education class and the topic was sex education. What they said was that if you were having sex with no protection it wasn't a matter of if you are going to get pregnant, it was a matter of when. That really hit me hard and then I was pregnant.

It was September and the first day of school. I should have been going back but instead I was getting on the city bus to go to a doctor's appointment. A male acquaintance from school was on the bus and he said to me "you sure are in good shape aren't you". I felt so much shame.

We moved into a small apartment and I quickly got into the role of housewife, calling my mom to ask how to cook an egg, keeping the apartment clean, and getting ready for my new baby. I started reading all the books I could on baby and child care. I remember thinking that I would be the most amazing mom in the world due to all the reading I was doing. Did I mention how naive I was?

The physical and emotional abuse started early in our marriage, while I was pregnant as I recall. He was very intimidated by my thirst for knowledge through books. He criticized me for needing to read all I could to prepare for our baby.

I gave birth to a baby girl, Tanya and of course she was my world. I loved taking care of her, dressing and bathing her. She was just so precious and cute. My daughter was born on the same day and in the same hospital as my mother in law who passed away at the same time from breast cancer. We stopped at the cemetery on our way home from the hospital on that chilly day in December of 1973 with my newborn all wrapped up in blankets. It was a bittersweet time and a very hard time for my young husband who had a good relationship with his mom.

My husband, who was the same age as me, was working as an Auto Mechanic. He was a hard worker and eventually got a job through my father working at General Motors.

The first number of years I don't remember a lot of the abuse. We lived two separate times in his dad's house, the first time he lived there with us and the second time we lived in his house on our own. His dad had quite a negative attitude and could be hurtful at times. My husband and his dad had occasional arguments. I mostly tried to stay out of their way.

Happier times were when we rented this little house for $185. per month. We had little money but life was okay. I planted a garden and made a nice home for us. I had my little girl and we spent our days together. I often took her to Storybook Gardens and she went on every slide in the park. They knew us at the grocery store by name as I was there every day with my daughter in her stroller. I was alone with my daughter a lot of the time, my husband would stay after work for a few drinks and he also spent time with friends outside of our home, partying, going on ski trips, golfing, etc. I spent a lot of my time going to the small branch library near our home and would get books to read to my daughter and a number of books for me (all self development type books) I tried to hide them from my husband because he would make fun of me and say things like "why do you need to learn this from a book". He would tell me that I was going to be brainwashed from all the books I was reading.

Tanya had just turned three when our son, Tyler, was born. Tyler was about 6 weeks old when our life was turned upside down. Tanya had a seizure and ended up spending 3 weeks in hospital. We soon found out that she had a rare genetic disorder that would affect her immune system. It was called Multiple Endocrine Disorder and her endocrine system was slowly failing her and breaking down.

It was after this time that we moved back into my father in law's house. He had moved out to live with his girlfriend so it worked out fairly well. We had some bad fights in this house and the Police were called on a number of occasions. My husband was detained overnight and I was so full of anxiety the next day when he was to come home. The cycle of abuse was in full swing though and he would come home very sheepish and apologetic, he didn't understand why he would hurt me, he loved me so much and would never do it again. Of course, I wanted to believe him and hoped that things would change. The honeymoon phase had begun.

Tanya was in school so I just had Tyler during the day. I started to volunteer at Childreach, a program for parents and their children, and I could bring our son with me. This started to open me up to what was out there in the world. I soon found out about a program called "Talking with Women" at the local branch library. I could take my son to the Preschool and I could be with some adult women. One day the Counsellor who was onsite was the speaker and she came to talk about what she was doing and how she could help people. I thought about it and then mustered up the courage to contact her. This turned out to be the best thing I could have done and was the first step in claiming my power back. I finally had someone to talk to who would listen and now knew what was going on. I remember leaving her office and crying my eyes out. I couldn't stop. I learned a new word that day and the word was oppressed.

My husband agreed to see this counsellor, however, he didn't like her and said that it was a "Feminist Women's Place" and he wouldn't go back. He was not pleased that I was seeing her but I persevered and was prepared to face the consequences.

The Counsellor invited me to attend an eight week Assertiveness Group which I later realized was a group for women who were abused by their partners. I was so full of anxiety before attending each week and was afraid to speak about what was actually going on in my home. I guess I thought if I speak about it, then I have to do something about it. I was so scared. I continued to see the Counsellor and she saw something in me that I didn't see. She saw that I was supportive and kind to others and that I was a leader. I started working with her as her assistant for 8 hours a week.

Even though this cycle of abuse was going on, and I was starting to get it, my husband and I purchased a house together out of town. I am sure he hoped I would be happy to be at home and less inclined to nurture friendships or to be involved with the community. Thankfully, I had gotten my drivers license by then so I could drive into the city to attend programs. We shared a vehicle though so that always had to be worked out first. The abuse cycle continued and was escalating. Because of the Police involvement my husband got involved with Changing Ways, a program for men who were abusive to their partners. He certainly felt that this made everything all right, but unfortunately it did not.

I started writing in a journal after every big physical and emotional blowout when he was passed out (from alcohol) and I knew he wouldn't wake up. I would read over the entries from the other times this had happened and through my tears all of a sudden I wrote "I NEED TO LEAVE". I had no idea how to do this. I had an eight hour a week job, no money saved, no car of my own, two kids (one with medical issues) who went to school in this small town and no place to go.

I attempted to leave on a few occasions only to go back after a few days to enjoy the honeymoon phase and then to feel the stress and anxiety and violence begin to escalate again. Each time I knew I would be going back as I had no concrete plan of what to do. I got a little stronger every time and took back a bit of my own power.

I finally did leave after 10 years together with only the children's beds and the television. I did not get any remuneration for my equity in the house. At the time I just felt like I couldn't fight it. It continued to be a hard time for a number of years after leaving as well. There was always conflict whenever there was visitation with the kids. I had to fight every month for a small amount of alimony.

At this time, I was working two days a week (16 hours) and I was on "Mothers Allowance" as it was called back then. I loved my job so much. I remember just feeling so blown away by what I was learning every day. I continued to read and learn as much as I could, signing up for courses at Fanshawe College and the University of Western Ontario.

For the 14 years after Tanya was diagnosed we spent a lot of time with doctor appointments, she had numerous blood tests, took a lot of medication a few times a day and we spent many hours in hospital both in London and in Toronto, Ontario. Our lives really just revolved around her. She was still a normal kid, was involved in many activities, and finished grade 12. She was such a go-getter, had a couple of jobs, was loved by her classmates and had many friends. The last few years of her life Tanya had many seizures and in one of my journals I counted 38. They were happening every few days or so and it was so hard to witness and to deal with. I fainted a couple of times, was on anxiety medication and just trying to do the best I could to get through my days. It was honestly the worst time in my life and it felt like a nightmare that was never going to end. The seizures were not easy for her to come out of. If they happened outside of our home, we usually ended up at the hospital. It was such a stressful time for us all. I always had hope that she would get better though. Tanya knew different and told me one night that she would soon be in the ground. In July of 1991, Tanya passed away at the age of 17.

I went right back to work after a short time off completely numb and not able to feel a thing. I attended a support group for Bereaved Parents but I wasn't engaged with it and didn't find it helpful. I had a big wall of protection around me and avoided my sadness for the most part. However, the sadness has always been there and never goes away. My life would have been so different if my daughter had lived and was here today. She was so much fun, so positive and just loved life. She loved young children and was so caring and compassionate with them. Tanya loved animals, especially cats. She loved school and learning, shopping, food and friends and family. I will grieve for her for the rest of my life.

I submerged myself in my work and I thoroughly enjoyed listening and supporting others through their own trials and tribulations. I felt so honored that others would trust me with their personal stories. I think it really helped me to forget about my own and to not focus on myself.

It's interesting how things evolve. While writing this chapter, my partner and I were entertaining the idea of moving. Because of that, I started pulling out boxes from the recesses of my closet.They had been forgotten, mostly just invisible. I started to take the time when I was alone to look at what was there. The boxes were full of my daughters collections, many photos, school projects, and letters that we wrote back and forth to each other. I started to go through everything and have gained some insights about our relationship which I wasn't really aware of when she was so young and having such a hard time. It often felt like it was about me and what I was going through at the time. Taking the time to acknowledge this painful time, after many tears and sadness has really felt very cathartic and healing for me.

I have always had a positive attitude and I tend to see the glass as half full 99% of the time. I am sure this has helped me so much with my work in mental health. I was so blessed to do this work for 38 years. When I began this work I was an Administrative Assistant and after a period of time I was able to get more hours and my job description changed to Community Support Worker. I often offered support to clients on the phone or in person if they dropped in and really had built up trust with them. I had gotten involved with support groups that were run by our program and by trial and error I participated and then became a Facilitator in my own groups. I was involved in Assertiveness, Self Esteem, Problem Solving and Parenting Groups.

I am one of the Founding Members of My Sisters Place which is a transitional program for women who are vulnerable, living on the streets, living rough or homeless, with mental health and addiction issues and struggling day to day. We worked on the plan for this new program for a couple of years before it came to fruition. We just couldn't believe we made this happen. I was seconded to work at My Sisters'

Place two afternoons a week when it first opened. I would show up at lunchtime and eat lunch with the women. We started connecting right away and building trust. It was all about the relationships. I started up a sewing program bringing in a sewing machine and having the women work on an individual piece which eventually became a small quilt. This still hangs at My Sisters' Place today.

After working in a Mental Health Program for 28 years, a one year contract opened up for a Community Support Worker at My Sisters' Place and I took the risk and applied. After one year of working in that role, the contract was extended and I worked there for ten more years before retiring. Well, actually semi-retired as I continue to love working with people. It was so amazing to be the first to get this grass roots organization off the ground. There were many trials and tribulations, two moves, we had daily meetings at the end of our days to debrief and it was the most meaningful work I ever did. "The work is dramatic and traumatic". These were words from the Director of Sistering in Toronto who we modeled our program after. I learned so much from all of the women I was in contact with there. This would include staff and participants and clients.

During my second year of working in this role I started working with a client who was dealing with her landlord due to the clutter in her apartment. I was intrigued and started reading as much as I could on Clutter, Chronic Disorganization and Hoarding. I decided to start up a Clearing Clutter Support Group. This group ran three to four times a year (8 week sessions) up until the pandemic hit. This work has inspired my life work and my business which is called "Space For You - Clear The Clutter, Heal Your Life". As you can imagine, I have taken many courses and workshops through Professional Organizers of Canada and also the Institute for Challenging Disorganization and read many books. I have helped hundreds of women and men to make progress in their homes and in their lives. I love helping my clients see what is beneath the clutter and might be holding them back. I help them to make positive changes in their lives and to make space for what is most important to them.

KIM TREMBLAY

~

Kim Tremblay has worked in the field of mental health for over 38 years. Kim started work as an administrative assistant and slowly became involved with co-facilitating and facilitating support groups and then supporting clients. She became passionate with helping clients to overcome Chronic Disorganization.

Kim is a Master Organizer and a Clutter and Hoarding Specialist. She has worked with individuals helping them clear the physical and emotional clutter from their lives since 2008. She founded and co-facilitated the Clearing Clutter Support Group which has helped hundreds of individuals to make positive changes in their homes and life.

Kim has a daily yoga and meditation practice and works on simplifying her own life. Kim supports and helps individuals to make more space in their homes and in their lives through Virtual Organizing. Kim lives in London, Ontario with her partner, Hallie and 14 year old grandson.

You can also find her here in her Facebook Group https://www.facebook.com/groups/DeclutterYourLifeandMind

You can find more information about Kim here http://spaceforyou.ca/

Sign up for a free 5 Day Declutter Your Life and Mind Challenge here http://eepurl.com/dsz4PP

12

~ SO IT IS

MARY GOODEN

~ **S**o It Is
I surrender - I release - I remember, this is my daily mantra. This is the energy I choose to live by.

How on "Earth" will this ever be possible? That thought is the smallest and largest obstacle in this lifetime.

We are brought into this world, for some as an achievement and others as a surprise or unplanned agenda. We are taught, guided, and coached based on the experience of others, which may also be known as "fact" hardwired, permanent ideas about everything and everyone. We are coached to fear the unknown and believe that "fact" surpasses all understanding. We are conditioned from the moment we take our first breath and for many until the last.

Where is the magic and mystery?

As children we feel it, before all the groundwork or raising is completed, we are playful and free to explore. When no one is looking we imagine our own facts, conditions, and beliefs. All too frequently we are criticized, punished, or medicated for the insatiable desire to discover a life that is extraordinary.

All of us are brilliant, bright, and beautiful!

We are all here to create something and to share our ideas and dreams with excitement, not for approval, comparison, or judgment. It all starts with a wish, a dream, or an intention to create something.

"This isn't the way I was taught"! Although clients, friends, family, and colleagues will bump into these words often, it is the spell that has been cast upon us, the constant pressure of performing to please someone else. I have stood alone for my beliefs in more ways than I can remember. I have sat paralyzed in anger, jealousy, guilt, and shame. In a desperate plea to feel better, we expect others to change. Each one of us has a pure and powerful purpose in the human experience. A mission to be compassionate and lead from the heart. This mission will ask you to choose surrender time and time again. Surrender is not giving up; it is the nature of letting in and allowing yourself to align with faith.

~ **Surrender**

So, this is where it all began. It wasn't a red flag, it was a rainbow flag, a wave of desire to be everything I came here to be. I was ready to stop accepting what I was choosing for me based on "fact", conditioned beliefs, striving for success, along with the expectations of others. I was done choosing guilt, shame and discomfort because I was conditioned to believe that this was the road to victory! It wasn't fun anymore living for a future that was recycled from the past! Victory is here and now, in the surrender! Would you believe me if I told you I have wings! Would you believe me if I told you that I can soar above the bullshit and create a life well lived! It looks and feels different than I thought it would because it is. You have heard it before, however, let me remind you, "If you want things to be different, do things differently"!

~ **Release**

I remember so clearly the night I sat by the gas fireplace, contemplating my reality. All of the opportunities and experiences that surrounded me were created by choice. At one time or another, each of them felt in alignment with who I was for that season. I believed that if just one were to fall out of place everything would, so I held on as tightly as I could. I often pondered on how much I trusted myself and my ability to hold it all together. Typical empowered female in the corporate climb, I proved I could do everything myself. I have held many labels, the energizer bunny, the master of all hats, and one of my favorites, the creator of time!

At the moment that the heat was rising on my backside, I felt it rising in my heart! I need more time, for me, for my children, for my relationships and most importantly for my mission. It all happened so quickly as if it had been decided before I could even make sense of the thought! I just had to choose it! I had to release, I had to let go.

I made the call that night, the decision to leap into uncertainty and surrender. My husband at the time was in the Navy, on a two-year tour in Japan. We had made the decision that the children and I would stay put in our Virginia Beach home. I excitedly emailed him to share the amazing adventure we had just been invited to take. I have always been one for adventure, trying new things and ideas for the sheer fun of it. I wouldn't be lying if I told you that this particular experience ended happily ever after, however a lot of shit hit the fan.

When I was a little girl everything in me wanted to be a star. My favorite shirt was royal blue with the most beautiful rainbow and a great big shining star. At this moment, I can still feel the joyful and free-spirited vibration that it carried. In essence, I wanted to feel just like that shirt, bright, colorful, and free. I was absolutely loved as a child and I truly felt the freedom to explore. My mother is the most loving human I know, and she was a terrific guide. I spoke my mind and my truth without hesitation, which didn't always resonate with my peers. I was not cold-hearted or vindictive, I was authentic and willing to stand up for myself and others. I had a lot of male friends, mainly because they were less gossipy and not judgmental.

I am an old soul; I have a deep reverence for love and truth. I took my first real step toward freedom when I was seventeen. I eloped with my high school sweetheart and moved to Virginia Beach, Virginia. I can honestly say, it was a really good run. We spent twenty-five years building our kingdom, societally known as the American Dream. We made it, big house, two kids, two cars and all the dazzle. If my things didn't own me, I am not sure who did.

The soul's mission is ever-evolving and my only way through was surrender. You have to be willing to let it all go in order to let it all in.

Just like that, I let it all go. Everything changed in what felt like the blink of an eye. I knew it would be one of my greatest adventures, so I said yes without knowing the details. In the beginning, we were all excited. We had a one-way ticket to New Orleans. I sold a lot of things including, the house, car, furniture, and anything else that wasn't nailed down. Liberation is a close second to the way this experience was feeling for me. I resigned from my corporate career (chaos), packed up my little's, and off we went into the deepest level of the journey.

You can fight it or invite it; everything is a choice. What I have discovered is, the mission will allow you to choose your beliefs, obstacles, desires, achievements, relationships, and destiny. I chose fun, play, travel, deeper relationships, and a deeper connection to my God's Divine will.

The "release" phase is lined with grace and gifts if you choose to see it in that way. "Ask and you shall receive", this invitation holds a lot of magic.

I asked to be released from old programming and the conditioning of working hard, paying taxes, and dying trying. Along with letter grades, external acceptance, and the life of the "Joneses" by my definition, "look at all the shit I have collected to look good, and I am too busy to enjoy any of it". I was thirty-seven when I shifted my perception of how I wanted to do and be in this life. I was thirty-nine when I signed the papers to end a marriage of twenty-two years.

I started this experience with a very traditional philosophy of marriage, "till death do us part". Did I do it on "purpose"? At first, I was bitter and resentful, I felt cheated, betrayed, and miserable. My response was pre-programmed, I fell right into what I call the human condition. This was my initiation and I am pleased to report, I SURVIVED!

Not a single one of us has the same mission and purpose. Especially, the one you have chosen to spend your life with. And then there is that "fact", my life partner, my soul mate, the very idea of "for better or worse, until death does us part" keeping you stuck in place, regardless of what you really want.

How long have you kept yourself small in order to please another, or because the human book of conditioning tells you to do so? Don't get me wrong, I believe in love and marriage, I have stood in the shoes of the bride twice! In fact, I am planning a third round of dress-up and nuptials with my beloved husband Richard in the sacred home of my soul, Sedona, Arizona. I believe in companionship! I believe that relationships build us up and break us down, is that the same thing? I came here to be different, to do differently. I am on a soul mission, a mission to love unconditionally, to ignite a fire in the hearts of humankind, a fire so hot that it purifies and sets free our very existence. Hearing this lights me up!

I take full responsibility for my decisions in this process. I release myself completely from the programming of regret. From these experiences, I take with me the memories of deep love and connection, along with the magic of my next-level mission. It was time to show up as the guide that my daughters needed me to be. They chose me to be their leader in the new world and I was ready to remember exactly how to do it.

~ Remember

The Universe is listening to everything that you think and say. I asked for fun and play when I set out on my New Orleans adventure and it absolutely delivered. I was finally invited to open a yoga studio, something I had been dreaming of for years. This space quickly became a stage to share my testimony and my teachings. Through every detail of divorce, custody battles, and disappointment, I managed to keep my head in the mission and share the very best of me. There were invitations to travel to all the places I had dreamed of and all the resources to make them a reality.

Can you guess the one place that created the most impact?

The moment my feet found the sacred land of Sedona I knew I was HOME. Richard and I spent a weekend immersed in the teachings of the Tao. This weekend was the catalyst that raised my vibration beyond anything I ever imagined possible. This land speaks in the voices of ancient ancestors, sacred storytellers, and ascending masters. If you sit in stillness long enough, you can feel her heartbeat align with yours. The calling to Sedona was a gift to me, for showing up, doing the work, and being the inspiration that is necessary to create lasting change in the world. I traveled back to this sacred land four times that year, each time anchoring in my reality of infinite possibility, creativity, and divine wisdom.

If you knew you couldn't fail, what would you leap into wholeheartedly?

What are you willing to let go of to be here now, to find joy now, to feel the ultimate peace that is already inside of you?

These are the questions that changed my life! I didn't immediately make a list; however, I did cast a vision.

How can I be of service for the greatest good of all?

I pray, I meditate, I ask the same question, "show me the way today, what is mine to share", and then I surrender, I release, and I remember.

I open myself up to be used as a living vessel of Christ's consciousness, love, and compassion. I remember who I came here to be!

To remember is to choose all of You.

Who am I willing to become!

Have you ever contemplated this very question?

Have you been the witness, the cheerleader, the lover, and the leader in your life?

I can share with you all the" how-to" books in the library but, if you don't do the work for yourself, you still won't completely understand the "how-to".

We are living this life together, collectively intertwined in the beautiful energy of love, peace, and freedom. Can you and I be vulnerable enough to accept these qualities, to release resistance, barriers, and blockages that have been created by circumstances that were meant to create growth and expansion in our life? Can we release from the conditioned perception and surrender to the true reality that is our nature, our God-given right to be whole, accepted, and loved unconditionally? In this place of vulnerability, self-acceptance, and compassion the soul speaks, the heart is heard, the veil is lifted, and our purpose is revealed. As the mind believes and accepts, the body receives and achieves!

Are you willing to show up fully in this life?

Are you open to receiving your gifts?

I completely cleared my plate, shut down the pity parties, and jumped in with both feet! One day at a time, one experience at a time, and one mantra or affirmation at a time. I created a practice of seeing only the gifts that existed in each circumstance. I let go of the idea that life was happening to me and chose to recognize that life is happening for me. Every single day I find stillness with God and the Divine Mother (nature).

I use all the teachings of my God, Yoga, Meditation, Breathwork, and Reiki to harmonize my being daily.

I practice being fully present in an all-encompassing way.

I acknowledge, accept, and align with the ineffable truth living in the deepest part of me, rather than being bound by hollow definitions and limited circumstances.

My vibration stays high and activates the vibration of others.

My teenage daughters are full of love and light and share that joy with their peers.

I aim to be the ripple effect, the very inspiration that I wish to see in the world!

My soul is completely aligned with limitless resources and opportunities and I say YES to every gift that my God shares with me.

I share the voices and victories of leaders, coaches, and visionaries all over the world through Divine Destiny Publishing.

I hold a loving and healing space for Soul Mastery, supporting those who are ready to surrender, release and remember.

I support the awakening heart's with soul-satisfying retreats in Sedona, Arizona.

I am wholeheartedly anchored into my soul's mission, and I wouldn't have it any other way.

I have nothing to lose and I give everything to love.

I remember who I came here to BE!

Are you ready to surrender, release and remember?

Ignite your fire Now!

MARY GOODEN

Mary Gooden is CEO and founder of Divine Destiny Publishing and Yoga Etc. She believes that abundance thrives in your ability to remain aligned and authentic, which is a daily practice. Mary has studied and practiced Yoga, Meditation, and Reiki Energy Harmonizing for almost 20 years. By taking an intuitive approach, she focuses on creating a space for clients to embody Soul-Mastery, a mentorship program that awakens you to your wholehearted mission.

Mary supports conscious visionaries, leaders, coaches, and entrepreneurs in becoming published authors by sharing their powerful message, story, and mission on a global platform. She has contributed to two #1 International Bestselling books and has created an International Bestselling book titled, Aligned Leaders. As a limitless source of God's Love and Light, her intention is to restore inner harmony, authenticity, and freedom to as many individuals as possible. Mary currently shares her time between Sedona, Arizona, and New Orleans, Louisiana with her husband and loving daughters.

- Website: www.yogaetcboutte.com
- Email: divinereikilove@yahoo.com
- Facebook: Divine Destiny Publishing
- Facebook Group Freedom, Ease & Abundance
- Instagram: @mjgooden76

13

FULFILLING LIFE-CHANGING GOALS
ROBIN RICHARDSON

"Let's face it; there are obstacles and challenges in every stage of our life." I tell myself this as a big lesson learned. We have tests from the moment of birth to the moment we transition at the end of this life. Some of them are left behind, and other tests seem to hang on as we travel along our path. My mother told the story of me barely surviving at birth. It wasn't an easy delivery. I was a breech. After delivery, she was exhausted, and I was nearly lifeless. I did not have the will to feed.

Mom said with certainty that I would not have survived if not for the tender loving care of a nurse. When that feeding moment happened, there were three beaming faces. My mom, dad, and the perfect nurse for me at that moment all joyfully knew I would survive. In their happiness, they shared the hope I would experience many more life challenges.

Now, I am 75, looking back at all life stages, wondering what comes next. Recently, I reflected on life while driving down a busy Aurora, Colorado street. Rather than being annoyed with the heavy traffic and other concerns, I felt at peace. Things like waiting for red lights to turn and being unhappy with impatient drivers honking long blasts of anger were not aggravating. My mind took me to a place of gratitude. I was thankful for all the thought, planning, execution, and public resources that went into making it possible for all of us to be traveling the road at that moment. There have been so many things thoughtfully done to make our life better. It feels good to reflect and appreciate the work of others. A job completed so we could have a better life. This thankful moment led to the notion of what comes next and how can I help others in need?

The blessing of life itself tells me the new challenge and achievement will depend upon my goals and execution. My wife and I are a team, and success will come from our work and capabilities. Thankfully, others can and will help. Lord knows we all need help. We also need to have the wisdom to understand the value of assistance when it is available. We need to recognize and choose with grace.

I must be honest, when you are 75, there are issues. There are limitations in health and expectations. My biggest issue has been an essential tremor condition, and it made the simple task of writing, signing my name on a restaurant ticket an embarrassing exercise. Thankfully, I have a sound mind and good health. Past life events have passed like a swift breeze and prepared me for future challenges.

From my kindergarten memory, learning to write the number 8 and singing London. Bridge then I fell to the ground with classmates. **We experienced the joy of play.**

Then, on to graduating from Ouray High School Class of 65. That is 1965 for those who are curious. **We learned the skill of making life transitions.**

I went on to earn a degree, studying World History from Fort Lewis College, graduating in 1971. **We knew the rewards of study.**

Many of us live in a country where we are allowed to explore and strive and fulfill our potential freely. That's my experience. As a student of history, I know it is not the case for everyone. There are many who have lived in a constant struggle, a battle, against the evils of racism and injustice. Still, it is a battle waged. Life is better as a result. I have seen in our society, new wonders of possibilities and the power of love revealed. I have hope the wonders of spirit will be captured and allow us to grow together in peace.

I have been extremely fortunate in the choices relating to friendship, marriage, and spiritual connections. After college, I returned to my roots working in a gold mine. My college degree did help as I moved into working as an industrial safety inspector and safety trainer in construction-related enterprises.

The greatest thing about my work experience has been the people I have met and the fantastic things I have learned. Skilled artisans working together and following a plan can achieve incredible outcomes completing complex jobs without suffering pain and injury and doing it on time. A sizable number of my life friendships have come from work connections, and those friendships reinforce my admiration for the power of challenging work.

On November 4, 1972, the single most significant event of my life happened in Norwood, Colorado, during a massive snowstorm. Kathy grew up in this little cow town, and we were married there in the Methodist church. In a flash of time, with the gift of our four daughters, we have flown forward like a capsule speeding through space. Another significant moment highlighting our little family's travel occurred in Grand Junction, Colorado March 22, 1979.

A small group, including my brother and a sister-in-law, participated in a simple exercise where we signed an enrollment card. At that moment, we became Baha'is and agreed to follow the loving guidance of the Founder, Baha'u'llah. It is impressive how choices such as the one we made on this day have impacted our world.

The thing I remember most about the event was a passage read. There is no formal process when you become a Baha'i, like a sprinkling or full immersion baptism. As mentioned, it is a simple exercise of signing an enrollment card. For my wife and I and the small group, it was casual. There were prayers spoken, stories told of what led others to discover and join, as well as expectations of the Faith explained.

Since there is no paid clergy, it is good to know the fundamentals, and that was a part of the discussion. What rings most clearly were the passages read. These passages, close to the hearts of our friends in attendance, added substance.

One passage went something like, and I am paraphrasing, *the reason we had made Choice to join the Faith was we had done a good thing for someone in need.*

Since that moment 42 years ago, during a simple enrollment after the reading of a passage, it has been my goal not to cause harm and to help others the best I can.

It has been a challenge to follow the guidance. It's difficult being honest, not judging others, not backbiting, not gambling, not using drugs and alcohol, only seeing the good in others, recognizing science and religion are connected, speaking the truth, accepting the equality of men and women, recognizing the power of diversity, as well as being committed to world peace. It seems like these amazingly freeing expectations are difficult maybe impossible to achieve. Yet, I have learned the more we visualize a result, the more likely the desired outcome will happen. The act of seeing, believing, and manifesting is the goal. Living up to these standards is a challenge rewarded with the comforting light of prayer and the promise there are more life stages after this one.

The method for success is to put together a plan that works for you. It requires using a system of trust, and the theme must ring true and be a part of you. Explaining the choices made and good fortune received that have carried me to this point in my life is the easy part of the story, and the hard part is putting together a a successful plan for my future.

There are nasty and nagging reflections that result in procrastination. I think we all experience them. We put off what needs to be done. The results are a roadblock. We feel a lack of confidence. An ugly sense of fear keeps us from moving forward. You may feel timid, believing things you have to say are boring and do not measure up. You could feel that you are letting the others involved in the project down by not doing your part.

All these negatives noisily rush in, crowding our brain space with one purpose: to stop progress. We all feel it, right? **I've found the one sure way to overcome the "Stop Progress" obstacle is you move forward.**

You start the motion. You bang away at the keyboard putting words together. You find the action of following your roughly constructed outline has, like magic, erased the obstacle and led to success. **It is all about action.** Trust, using intuition and thoughtful actions, we find the spiritual gifts within can move us forward. Yes, even at 75, I have learned we continue to face the emotion of fear. It is a challenge that does not go away. Letting us know we are not finished with our mission. There is more to be done.

So, let me explain the system I developed. The one formed to make my future into a reality. For me, the plan-building exercise usually starts in the morning and goes something like the following:

In the process of removing a feeling of being hammered with doubt, I wake with the knowledge this would be the day I complete my work in writing my Chapter. I open my eyes, blinking, allowing the morning focus to take shape. An unobstructed vision is critical for the task ahead. I close my eyes and think of my three goals for the day. Oh yes, shopping with Kathy and exercising at the YMCA. The first two can be achieved without much planning; nothing special is needed. The third is the big challenge of writing the Chapter. As I mentioned, success requires action. Kathy has already gone downstairs.

The bed is mine. I toss off covers, get the blood flowing with sit-ups and leg kicks. Feeling revived, I calm myself by breathing and closing my eyes. I consider my system of offering three thanks for the day. The three things I am grateful for this morning. **"Let's see..."**

1. Being alive and able to move.
2. Checking out the sunshine coming through the window and enjoying another day with Kathy.
3. The Chapter, the opportunity to write The Chapter.

I make the bed and sit for a moment. Then I say my morning prayer. It is refreshing and straightforward with the following words:

> I have wakened in Thy shelter, O my God, and it becometh him seeking that shelter to abide within the Sanctuary of Thy protection and Stronghold of Thy defense. Illumine my inner being O my Lord, with the splendors of the Dayspring of Thy Revelation, even as Thou didst illumine my outer being with the morning light of Thy favor.

This awakening has taken no more than 10 minutes and led into my morning meditation. It is a meditation method that brings the steps of my creative effort together. I have chosen this vision structure because of trust, and I know it works.

I follow the practical guidance of my Faith. I discovered four qualities the Founder loved to see in other people. **It is these four qualities I have built into my success vision.** Once again paraphrasing, **the four qualities are:**

1. Enthusiasm and courage.
2. A face wreathed in smiles and a radiant countenance.
3. Being able to see with your own eyes and not through the eyes of others.
4. And blessed with the ability to carry a task once begun through to its end.

The meditation is like a movie, and I picture myself filled with enthusiasm and courage. I am smiling and glowing with an aura of light. Feeling marvelous, standing tall, supported by a firm structure made of truth. My eyes are vibrant, connecting the outside world with the spirit within. I see myself carrying a shovel and pick and know, without question, these tools represent the work required for the job before me. I know to my core; the Chapter will become reality with my best and most honest effort. It will be a job based on my understanding. I am in no way harassed, bullied, or intimidated to follow the path of someone else. I speak the truth as the finished product is revealed. I repeat the vision, feeling courage, filled with happiness, seeing with my own eyes, and recognizing the completed job by picturing the title of my Chapter: Fulfilling LifeChanging Goals at 76. In a flash of light, the letters appeared along with the meaning. In the process of visualizing success, taking on a feeling of joy, allowing deep breaths to saturate my lungs with oxygen, I attach my new goals preparing for the age of 76.

Kathy and I have not secured a generous sum in our bank account. We know we need to bring more money into our lives. This knowledge is ok, and it is a gift. We are thankful to be capable and blessed with the health, means, and capacity to meet our needs.

We are breaking the mold of retirement and achieving more at this age than in any other stage of our life. We have things to gain and the tools to make it happen. We are also thankful to have family and friends to help us along. This is such a fantastic time to be alive and learn new skills. We move forward into life possibilities with a positive attitude, an abundance of good health, good friends, good family, and sound spiritual guidance. We use the tools of our past and vision for the future as the framework for success.

Our new goals for the year 76 include:

1. Successfully selling goods and services using eCommerce systems and proven money-making platforms.
2. Use our love for writing to generate and publish low-content journals, eBooks, and paperbacks with the Kindle Amazon platform.
3. Recognizing life is not all about money, we press on to improve our physical health. It is critical at our age to maintain the energy needed to meet our goals.
4. Grow a more significant presence in the business world. We think we can burst the bubble going into unfamiliar territory. Vigilant for new opportunities and expanding our team using a welcoming attitude of support will lead to success.

As with all things, it takes challenging work and support from others to learn the skills needed to create a successful business. Work, spiritual truth, focused visualizing (courage, happiness, seeing with your own eyes, and a completed job) clear the path for Kathy and my winning ways. Our business is built on the principle of living a positive life. We are committed to saying prayers, listening to the joyous chatter of children for inspiration, and experiencing the music of the moment to nourish our brains.

We love and enjoy the company of family. We are gaining greater realization for the potential greatness of people working together. A welcoming, supportive attitude is the key to building a team. We recognize the power of diversity and have come to love the many life stages we have been given.

This Chapter ends with a question. It is the same question posed when we started the Chapter. What comes next, and how can we help others in need?

We now know finding the answer is realized by acting, trusting in spiritual guidance, and bringing to life a loving attitude of service.

ROBIN RICHARDSON

~

Robin Richardson is a 75-year old man who loves to explore his past and share a belief in the power of unity.

He grew up in Ouray, Colorado in the San Juan Mountains. In this little town where he learned about mining and the art of seeing gold. He spent many hours in Ouray's natural hot water swimming pool looking up at the peaks, putting words to it all, being guided to a love for writing.

His wife Kathy and four daughters have pushed forward with a positive desire to experience the best in life. His family experience and work in the energy field has provided a reservoir of writing information. Robin and his wife Kathy have known there is a light within and being Baha'is provides a unique spiritual perspective. In his writing, he explores where goodness, kindness, and love can take us.

Writing is a beautiful tool to make our shared experience possible.

You can find my eCommerce website at: https://robkatmkt.com

14

COMING HOME

SILKE HARVEY

The plane touched down at Sofia airport. It was late at night and the air was still balmy and warm. What a difference to the heavy rain and cold I'd left behind at Liverpool airport! The flight had been pleasant enough. I stepped off the plane with great excitement for the adventure that lay ahead. From the airport, I went straight to a nondescript hotel, a typical affair, not much different from any airport hotel you'll find anywhere in the world. There were no connecting trains or buses to Vratsa on the same night, so I had pre-booked a hotel to start my stay in Bulgaria. After an evening pleasantly spent sampling some very tasty Bulgarian cuisine and chatting to Shawn on Messenger, I dozed off contentedly in the comfortable hotel bed. I got up the next morning with anticipation. Here I was in Bulgaria, speaking not a single word of Bulgarian. Yet, I had to somehow catch a train from Sofia to Vratsa.

I'd done my research and it looked straightforward: Sofia Central Station to Vratsa Central Station, one train, no transfers. I decided to take a taxi to the central station, easing myself into the situation by not attempting to buy a ticket for the metro and finding my way with every sign in an alphabet and language I didn't understand. I arrived at the central station and somehow managed to purchase a ticket to Vratsa.

The fact that everything was written in Cyrillic didn't help. With a bit of time to spare until the departure of the train, I decided to go for some breakfast in a little cafe outside the train station. The place was a throwback to the 1980s. In fact, most of what I'd seen of Sofia so far reminded me very much of Duesseldorf, the city where I'd grown up in the 1980s. I sat down at an old wooden table on an old wooden chair with a red and white checkered wax cloth covering the table, fake flowers in a little plastic vase, a Coke machine in the corner, and a table full of menus that I had no way of reading. Thankfully there were pictures of the dishes and I ordered what I thought looked like breakfast. I ended up getting a rather strange mixture of breakfast, lunch, and brunch rolled into one. It tasted pleasant enough. The whole nostalgic scene was accompanied by Wham on the radio. I'd not heard that kind of music on the air for I don't know how long. Wham was followed by Europe, was followed by Madonna, was followed by other songs that had been around thirty to forty years ago – I felt at home. I still remember cafes like this from when I was a teenager in Germany. The owner of the place was very nice and even though he didn't speak a word of English, we managed to somehow understand each other.

I paid and left for my train – negotiating the large central station was an art in itself. It took me ages to figure out that the platforms were underground and how to get to the main part of the station. But I'd managed to figure out how the word "Vratsa" looked in Cyrillic because on the timetables, thankfully, everything was written in both Cyrillic and Latin letters. I managed to get to the correct platform and board the right train. The journey was another trip down memory lane. I found myself in the 1980s rolling stock from Germany's national railway company, which apparently Bulgaria had bought up at some point. These were the compartments I'd travelled in so many times as a child. Even the seat covers were still original. The train passed through some breath-taking scenery whilst I was listening to the old ladies next to me happily chatting away in a language I didn't have a clue about.

When we came to a stop, I almost thought we were in Vratsa already but it turned out to be a false alarm. The place was a stopover. By looking out of the window – yes, you could still actually pull down the old sash windows and nobody stopped you from sticking your head out

– I could see that half of the train was being uncoupled and re-coupled to another locomotive. Now I was worried because I knew from experience that if this train was being uncoupled, half of it was going to go off into another direction. So the big question was: which half of it went to Vratsa? My half? Desperate to get some answers, I used Google Translate to ask the old lady next to me if I was on the correct train to Vratsa. She answered excitedly, chattering away with great animation. I could just about make out a word that sounded very much like "Angliski". I understood that she was asking me if I was English, so I said yes. Suddenly, the old lady jumped up and shouted something into the compartment, repeatedly using the word that I believed to mean "English". I think she was asking if anybody in the compartment spoke English because an old guy stood up and in broken English said to me that yes, he spoke a little English and that he would tell me when it was time to get off the train in Vratsa. I thought it very endearing how the old lady had immediately tried to help, even though we couldn't communicate with one another. I thanked her profusely and she understood. We spent the rest of the journey smiling at each other, even though we couldn't speak a word. When the train pulled into the outskirts of Vratsa, the old man got up to tell me that it was time to get off the train. Suddenly the whole compartment jumped up and everyone started shouting goodbye, waving and laughing. That was one of the nicest moments I'd ever experienced on any train journey. These people were warm-hearted and friendly to a stranger they'd never seen before.

I was picked up at the station by the estate state agent and whisked to a comfy hotel where I spent the next few days whilst I was sorting out the formalities of the purchase of our house that Shawn and I had just recently won on eBay. On the third day, it was finally time and the deed was registered in my name. I was the proud owner of the keys to my own Bulgarian country home. The estate agent took me to the place. It would have been just too complicated to get from Vratsa to our little village on public transport without knowing the language. I was taken in a lovely Jaguar car, feeling like a queen in the backseat. As we drove on, the countryside turned greener and lusher by the minute. It was the first week of March and I was surprised at how much nature had already started to wake up and at how mild and warm the weather was. It was a real shock to the system after spending the last few years in the cold climate of the North East of England. Here we were on the tenth of March and it was twenty degrees already! After a little while, we turned off the main road and drove towards a small village.

The road gradually got worse, with potholes the size of sinkholes appearing in the most unlikely of places. Suddenly, we started meeting horses and carts on the road. This was like something you'd read in books. When we got to the village, the driver slowed down because he had trouble finding the property. We turned off the road onto a dirt track, which I later found out is the main road and part of the village infrastructure. We carefully rolled down a path that looked not much better than a hiking trail in the UK, making our way past old houses, dodging chickens in the road, upsetting cats, sheep, and goats, and even annoying a cow. I admired the driver for keeping his cool amidst this menagerie. At the end of a dirt track where it looked like we could go no further, he consulted his satnav and took a sharp right turn into a field. There was no road at all but he didn't seem the slightest bit concerned. He slowly and expertly maneuvered the Jaguar across a meadow, away from the last houses. I was getting a little worried by now because the last thing I'd expected was to go off-roading in a luxury car.

After taking another right in the field, we got to some houses and gates. The estate agent told me, "There you are. This is your house." We were standing in a field surrounded by cows, horses, and sheep. I'd bought a house that didn't even have road access. Later on, I found out that this is quite normal in Bulgaria and that the field is officially classed as a road and our address has a proper street name and number. The estate agent showed me how to open the gate, which was another art. After giving me all the keys and showing me what was what, she left me there and told me she was going to pick me up in four hours. She even gave me some food and drink. I went inside and saw my new, old house for the very first time. This day has burned itself into my memory as the most magical of my life.

As I walked in through the gate, I entered a different world. To the right of me were two dilapidated barns. You could see that one used to be a stable with a hayloft. The other one had been used either for chickens or pigs. To the left was an old garage. When I walked through a second gate ahead of me, a fairytale scene unfolded itself in front of my eyes. To the right of me was a beautiful witch's cottage and ahead of me my very own Villa Villakula. I felt like Pippi Longstocking exploring my domain. The garden was surrounded by mature trees. There was so much green everywhere! I started wandering through the grounds. The very first thing I noticed was the benevolent feeling everywhere. From the moment I'd stepped through the gate, I could feel that this was a good place. I was surprised to find out that despite the long trip through the field to what seemed the other side of the moon, the house was surrounded by neighbors on three sides, all hidden away behind trees and shrubs. So it wasn't quite as lonely and deserted as I'd first thought.

I'd expected to feel a little spooked going into this old and long-abandoned place that was new to me – entirely on my own with nobody for company but myself and my thoughts. But as I started exploring, the feeling of warmth, friendliness, and benevolence was getting stronger and stronger. I looked in all the old barns but decided to leave them for another time as the cobwebs and spiders were pretty impressive. I didn't fancy any close encounters without a broom. With each outhouse and building, I was entering, my excitement grew because everywhere I found artefacts and mementos of a life that had once been lived here. I knew from the deeds that this house had been owned by one family since it was first built in the 1950s. I found signs of that life everywhere and it looked like a good life. Apparently, the old people had died and for a while, the children had still used the place as a holiday home. But now, they were also getting older and the grandchildren had no further interest in the old homestead, living in the city and leading completely different, modern lives. So they'd sold the place with all of its contents. It was like a time capsule. There were artefacts from a time gone by, ranging from the 1950s to the modern day, from the old treadle sewing machine and radiogram right through to modern posters on the wall. The house itself looked every bit as magical as in the photos the estate agent had sent: crooked, charming, a little bit wonky around the edges but perfect. An old coal range was standing outside in the yard. I later found out that that's where the Bulgarian people used to cook. The old country folk didn't like indoor kitchens because of the dirt they make, so they would cook outdoors in all weather. The house was divided into an upstairs and downstairs, with the downstairs being a semi-basement.

I decided to go into the basement first. I expected it to be spooky and to even be a little scared or unnerved. But the strangest thing happened. As I opened the door, a benevolent wave of happiness engulfed me, a feeling of coming home. I had a distinct feeling that the house was welcoming me. And even though the basement was dark and very damp and unlived in for many years, I didn't once feel scared or anxious. I walked through all the rooms, fascinated by this time warp. I found that upstairs was the same. As I opened the door, I again felt like I was coming home. I had this feeling like I'd always been in the house. Everything felt familiar yet new – very curious indeed.

After a while, I decided to have a break. It was very warm and I was sweating and thirsty. I drew up an old, rickety chair by the coal range in the yard. I was sitting quietly, munching on a croissant and drinking some lemonade. The bees were buzzing and a cow was mooing somewhere in the village. It was answered by a chorus of sheep. I was taking in the wonderous view from my huge garden across the field I'd come through. It was a peaceful and idyllic moment and a scene worthy of a painting. I couldn't believe that this was all mine. I couldn't believe my luck. I thanked my heart profusely for giving me this gift – for encouraging me to buy a house simply because I loved the look of it, without ever seeing it or knowing the country even – and was glad that I'd listened to its advice. I was completely relaxed. The sun was hot, the insects were still buzzing and I was on the verge of dozing off when all of a sudden, I heard footsteps. I knew that I was entirely on my own. I also knew that I'd locked the front gate. There was no way that the estate agent could have been back early and surprised me. At this point, I should have been scared, but the strange thing was that I was more curious than anything else. I got off my chair and turned around. The sound of the footsteps had come from upstairs. I looked up to the big living room window and there she was: an old lady in a traditional Bulgarian headscarf and knitted cardigan was standing at the upstairs window waving at me, appearing so happy to see me. I waved back thinking, "How did this old lady get in? She must be a neighbor."

I got up and walked upstairs. The house was empty. I walked into the living room where I'd seen her standing at the window... Nothing – absolutely nothing. I knew then that my first instinct had been right. The owner of the house, the old lady, had welcomed me. Later on, when I looked through some of the personal belongings and photographs left in the old place, I found out that this old lady was indeed the lady of the house. She'd fallen in love with this gorgeous boy. It looked like a true love affair. He appeared to be a Russian soldier who married his Bulgarian sweetheart and built the house with his own hands. The family lived in the old homestead until the old lady, who I later found out is called Maria, passed away in the 1990s. She was the last one who permanently lived in the house.

I've had many visitations from Maria since. She's turned into one of my Spirit Guides. She often counsels me and gives me good advice, even when I make business decisions. I know that somewhere, somehow, we're related in time and space. I'm not sure how, but maybe one day I'll unravel this mystery. I've met Maria on many shamanic journeys and I know that she's the one who called across the Universe for me and my husband to buy the property. She wanted us to have it and she made it happen. Because she knew that I am a like-minded soul, a sister, who would love the house as much as she did. She also, later on, welcomed Shawn when he was pottering in the garden. One day, he noticed a piece of paper blowing at his feet. When he picked it up, it was a funeral notice. They're very common in Bulgaria and they usually get put up in public places where they stay until they rot away from the wind and weather. This sheet of paper was from 1993, yet it was in almost perfect condition. There's no way it could have ever hung outside for such a long time. So how it blew at Shawn's feet in the garden is a mystery to this day. The picture on this funeral notice was the very woman I'd seen in the window waving at me. It was the same lady, the same clothes. That's how I found out that she's called Maria.

I now know that this house was always meant for us. Some things in life are simply meant to be and we have to accept them for what they are. Explanations are futile. We're spiritual beings and we must acknowledge ourselves as such. If we open our minds to Spirit and we truly listen without putting up barriers, without prejudice and doubt, we start getting deep insights and a wealth of knowledge and life will be so much better for it. The Universe will reward us with untold inner riches if we accept that there's more to our existence than meets our three-dimensional human eyes. This deep knowing serves me well in all areas of my life – from private to business and anywhere in between. When I need to find an answer to a question, when I'm unsure which way to turn, I consult my team of spirit guides. Maria is always with them now. Her advice has never let me down. When I see and hear her, I know I've come home.

SILKE HARVEY

~

Silke Harvey is the founder of the Inner Hippie Club and Inner Hippie Books, a radio presenter, Reiki Master, Reiki Drum practitioner, Chakra Dancing facilitator, and HAO Animal Healing graduate.

She uses her energy healing skills to help women release their Inner Hippie, that carefree teenage feeling before life got serious, and her translating and editing skills and passion for books to publish powerful stories of inspiring women.

In the past, she toured all over the UK and Europe as a bass player in various Rock n Roll bands, ran an indie record label, and developed a successful career in financial translation working for one of the Big Four, then freelancing it.

Silke lives in the UK with her husband and beloved rescue dog and splits her time between her cosy home near the coast and her beautiful country cottage in Bulgaria where she is planning to run retreats.

Connect with Silke

- www.innerhippiebooks.com
- www.innerhippieclub.com
- https://bbsradio.com/innerhippieclub

15

SIMPLE SPIRITUALITY...AN ACT OF SELF-LOVE.

SIMRAN BHATIA

"When is this FedEx truck going to get here?" I turn back from the window directing the rhetorical question to my husband. "Waiting at the window isn't going to make it get here faster. Don't you constantly talk about divine timing?" he responds. What a dose of my own medicine. I feel my left eyebrow raise up and make a mental note of how obnoxious it must sound when I give him these kinds of responses, even though it's the truth.

I'm totally aware that the universe operates on its own perfectly orchestrated schedule, that I don't have any control over. The only thing in my means is to shift my own vibration. So I take a deep breath and guide everyone to the family room for a little family bonding time with the kids before we get them ready for bed. As we sink to the floor and tickle each little one running by and revel in their laughter, something magical happens... the phone for which I've become impatient to arrive lands on our front porch. But I am in the present moment so I don't notice until I pass by the door on my way ushering the kids up to brush their teeth. And because I've shifted my vibration I'm able to wait patiently till later to even open it.

Instead of rushing to get out the new phone, which is going to replace the one my almost 2-year-old broke two days before, I sit with the box in my hands and give myself the space to reflect. My thoughts began at the last phone unboxing six months prior, which felt so odd because I'd had the same phone for years before that. But my parents had gotten me a Christmas gift and I was practicing receiving in a new way, so I had accepted.

My thoughts then filter through the last month... a situation I was really unhappy about at work, and getting such a bad cough after that I lost my voice during Mercury Retrograde, and a few days after I recovered my phone broke. I normally have an unusually easy relationship with Mercury Retrograde compared to the stereotypes throughout the spiritual community, but this one had really taken a frying pan and beat me over the head.

I think over the text messages I'd exchanged with my go-to energy healer/transformation coach that I was working with daily at the time... and how I'd told her I just wasn't ready to fully express my thoughts yet to anyone because I was trying to let my wounds surface this time, so she could help me heal them, instead of my rationalizing and intellectualizing them.

And I had finally come into my own growth in that process. I realized in the process of not being 'able' to talk, that I had silenced my ability to do so. So that everyone around me would stop pushing me for a story, or an answer, or to react. Not ironically the day I fully accepted my own decision about how I was going to move forward in the situation, my toddler looked me in the eye and smiled as she grabbed my phone, ran off and stuck her wet hands into the charging port.

A few hours later when my phone wouldn't charge anymore I came to the conclusion that as usual she was forcing me into a situation where I'd need to up-level. I'd learned now in my interactions with this beautiful little soul that she was here to push me into reclaiming my personal power.

So what better symbolism for the need to communicate in a new way than a new phone? And I saw the message that with this new phone I needed to experience an even bigger up-level than I had already been engaging in over the past six months with the first new phone. As I acknowledged the insight that had entered my mind, I was taken back to March 2020. The infamous month the COVID-19 pandemic shutdown schools all across the United States.

We began enrolling beta testers for the Flowation Marketplace between March 1st and 11th. The 12th was supposed to be the last day of school before my son's two week spring break, and beta testing was supposed to start the day he went back. An hour after he got home that day my phone pinged with an email notification from the school saying it was shut down until further notice, and would be moving to remote learning after the break. I slumped down to the sofa, dropping my hand that still held my phone to my right side.

Remote learning for a three-year-old? With a 6-month-old in the background? *How* was that going to work? My head dropped down and my shoulders slumped further as I exhaled like a rag doll. I knew my husband would pitch in with handling the kids, but I also knew given the circumstances of our work situations that I would end up carrying more hours than him on the weekdays. So *how* was I going to manage a round of beta testers at that time?

A few moments later I forced myself to get up, straighten out my spine and push back my shoulders. I had a reputation for being good in crisis and I already knew I was going to to-do list my way through this situation. The model our society holds up of being a productive leader or entrepreneur is often steeped in masculine energy. Being someone who thinks and reacts quickly, and has instantaneous decisions and solutions to problems. Without realizing it at the time my entire system had defaulted back to the masculine model I'd been taught my entire life. I had spent the years since my son's birth de-conditioning myself from these lessons. But there was something about all of our childcare options shutting down as our customers were expecting a big unveiling of our new service, that sent my adrenaline levels through the roof and had yanked the rug right from under my decision-making process. Back again in the present moment I cringed slightly at the memory of all the decisions I made in the following two months that with hindsight I can now label as mistakes.

They all fell in one big category - people-pleasing. Sometimes I wish I could just burn that version of myself down to the ground. I look down at the tattoo inside of my left forearm that says "love yourself," sigh, and silently forgive myself for the thousandth time for defaulting to a way of doing things that I had been taught from birth. Compassion for all versions of myself has become a necessary part of life as an entrepreneur, especially as one who seems called to new business ideas that are disruptive to the way people are normally doing things. It's an area of entrepreneurship that is ripe with failure until you finally hit the tipping point on a viable idea that can actually turn into a business.

As I conclude the 'forgive yourself' ritual I slip back into the past. Remembering how luckily three months into the pandemic I had started to come back to my senses, and started stripping away the unnecessary things that were adding to my stress level and throwing me totally out of balance. The things that didn't add to my children's happiness, my mental health, or the vision I was trying to achieve with my company. I chose my priorities for life and work all over again, in light of our current childcare circumstances. I wanted to nourish my children so they could thrive despite all of the fear they were suddenly surrounded by. And I wanted to get to the other end of the tunnel on this business idea- it was perhaps my most important ever out of all the businesses I had run in the last 18 years. And I wanted to focus on quality in my few close relationships over quantity, so I was open with my husband, friends and family on how much I could handle giving to our relationships with our children being so young, and my business being at such a critical phase in the middle of what felt like the world falling apart.

Letting go of so many "shoulds" that were wrapped up in the very essence of how our society believes women are supposed to be ... created spaciousness in my mind. So I could approach work with a new sense of clarity. And as the summer months of 2020 began, so too began my journey from solo entrepreneur to CEO. And a transformation of observing all the shadows in myself where I was still operating from a limiting belief.

I had spent the last almost 4 years telling myself that my decision to have limited work hours, so that I could be present with the kids was the thing that caused this intrinsic struggle I experience each day between 'did I get enough done at work?' and 'am I being present enough with the kids?" I had always led large teams my entire professional career, and with it came a kind of quiet fatigue from the pace of juggling so many personalities. And having started this particular business before my first pregnancy had given me the welcome relief of being totally on my own clock. I was experiencing flow daily without the stress of all the conflict-resolution and project management that comes with a team. The first thing I had to acknowledge was that the amount of hours I had to work had nothing to do with the conflict in my mind. It was actually a clash between being an entrepreneur who had found their calling and would rather be at work than doing other things. And because I wanted to be at work, I had fallen in a nasty trap of thinking I had to do everything myself. It left me with the question mark each day of whether I had accomplished enough in the hours I had limited myself to. And voila you have the conundrum almost every Mompreneur who is running her business *around her kids* ends up facing - all your progress is in the fashion of three steps forward, and one step back.

I began the month of July with a renewed desire to heal this conflict within myself because I knew there was nothing left to strip away in my life, except the tasks in my business that could be better handled by someone else. At the time I had a sense of looming discomfort around the need to bring people into my business, and to make this shift away again from being the one who did all the things, to the one who makes sure all the things happen. I was almost certain that a certain lesson I'd always struggled with was going to rear its ugly head. I mean I couldn't possibly expect to openly be a spiritual small business coach transitioning to spiritual software services provider without expecting my karma to smack me in the face a couple of times, right?

"Are you actually going to set up the phone, or just stare at the box all night?" My thoughts are interrupted by my husband walking into the room. I chuckle softly as he continues, "let me guess, you're thinking about the last phone, and how it was a sign at the time, and now this one is a sign." "Ummhmm" I say, "Don't worry, I'm not going to make a habit out of getting a new phone every time I up-level. I think I got the point this time. I hope..." He laughs and shakes his head at my last words as he walks out the door knowing full well that I am so obsessed with my own evolution and growth that we'll be talking about the same lesson in a few months from a totally different angle.

Which is exactly what my mind ponders now. Did I really get the point? Or was I still missing something in this lesson that had been playing itself out since last October? As I open the box and pull out the phone I'm surprised by how lightweight it is compared to the last phone. My mind flashes back to the same realization 6 months ago before putting on the protective cover. And my thoughts begin to ping-pong.

First I'm struck by the parallel that communicating used to feel lighter, before I had begun to hire the team and felt like I had to communicate so many boundaries on an almost hourly basis. Doing that was a necessity though to address the looming fears I'd had going in, that I'd repeat my age old mistake of people-pleasing even with my own employees and contractors to the extent then when someone wasn't performing or made a mistake I'd blow past it at the cost of the business in an effort not to upset anyone else.

But then I reflect on how learning to communicate those boundaries early often meant I didn't have to suffer the mental anguish later when someone unknowingly was playing bumper cars with my boundaries. Or the sleepless nights over deciding to let go of multiple team members. Fixing those situations was much more emotionally taxing. My mind then wanders to the lessons I've assimilated over the last six months since picking up that last phone. The one my parents offered to gift me the night after I finally let go of some team members who weren't operating with the integrity that I wanted people to embody as representatives of my company's brand. The phone that I took as a sign that while the decision felt excruciating to confront them, was clearly a step in the right direction for my soul.

Thinking back on my question to myself of whether I've fully learned my lesson. I give myself some credit. I better understand my responsibility now as the leader of this company, that I have to have foresight in each moment. It has become regular practice now for me to ask myself "is this a situation where if I articulate a boundary now, or slow down my decision-making process, I will save everyone a headache later?"

And over the past month I was finally getting comfortable enough in my skin to change how things were done, adding a lot of pause to my decisions, a layer of divine femininity into my decision making process. The space for ALL of the relevant details to fully make themselves known, the space for conclusions to fully gestate before being announced, and to birth new ideas in a more patient way. But even with all the growth that I was now actually embodying I was troubled by the fact that my communication now also felt like it was weighed down like my last phone with the protective cover, always fraught with the risk of over-thinking how to communicate the *why* behind each decision properly.

I let myself internalize this realization deep into my consciousness.

And a question floats to the surface of my mind. I had given myself the permission to let my intuition lead my decision making, so why wasn't I letting it lead my communication with others? I feel the energetic weight that question creates in my body, and then sigh deeply as I connect the new phone to the charger and prepare to end the night. I'm scared of something, but I can't put my finger on just what it is. So like every night as I slip under the covers I set an intention for my Guides to bring me clarity- how could I approach this need for foresight, and communicating that foresight, with a lighter energy? This ritual for me each night is practice surrendering to the Universe, allowing a sign, symbol or some inspired thought to lead me to the answer easily.

The next morning I quietly sneak downstairs to the kitchen and give gratitude for the electric kettle that is warming my tea. With two kids five and under, I silently give gratitude for everything in my life that allows me to multitask, or care for myself with little effort. I begin the short walk downstairs to my home office, and as I enter my eyes fall on the new protective cover sitting on my desk that had arrived the day before the phone. I wrinkle my nose, feeling resistance at all the weight it will add to my new phone, and passively decide to ignore putting it on for a bit. Instead, I login to the Flowation Community and look at the coaching questions I need to respond to for the day.

I read the first question off of my screen, "What can I do to find a way to be more spiritual when I am looking at business? The world doesn't seem to work on a spiritual mindset." Hmm. I pick up my mug and hold it in both hands, then close my eyes and take a deep relaxing breath. I relish the sense of security I'm flooded with. I can feel my nervous system calming down. And then I ask myself, what does this person need to hear? I fall into my 6 year old habit of channeling the information my coaching clients need to hear instead of relying on just my intellect. While sometimes I'm even surprised by the way things come out it always seems to resonate with them and touch them deeply enough to begin the transformation process. As I reflect on this thought I'm struck by the obviousness of the answer I asked for last night. I don't need to figure out every single detail of the communication I'm having within my team or potential Flowation customers. I can channel what everyone needs to hear, just like I always have with my coaching clients. I squint my eyes as I'm struck with the realization that worrying so much about how to communicate my boundaries and decisions is still an act of people-pleasing. And this is just yet another layer in the onion of this lesson, and the process of unraveling the impact my limiting beliefs are having on my reality.

    I take another clearing breath and smile as I look at the protective cover to my left and sense my reluctance to slip it on my phone has melted away. As I tell my coaching clients, just a two millimeter paradigm shift can change your entire reality. And you can turn something as ordinary as opening a phone box into a life-size epiphany that drives your transformation forward. This is the secret sauce to running a business from a spiritual-perspective. Letting every moment be your teacher, so that you don't require a crisis. Though sometimes we do need to lose our voice to find how to use it in a different way. There is no shame in the lessons you are presented or in the way you learn them. The only goal is to keep showing up and learning.

SIMRAN BHATIA

Simran Bhatia is the Founder of Flowation.com a Marketplace for spiritual-minded professionals to sell their goods, services, and more. Flowation provides them with business software and resources to manage their business, and grow it to the next level. And a private community with Coaches and Experts on many topics that provide free coaching and advice.

Simran has a unique blend of spiritual practice and depth of business experience. She has been in the publishing, e-commerce and marketing industries since 2003, and actively worked with healers of all modalities since then. She is an attorney who worked mostly with small business owners in her former law practice.

Not an entrepreneur? You can still sign up for the Flowation Community at www.flowation.com to join in our monthly networking events, and interact with the spiritual-minded community you wish you were surrounded by.

16

ABOUT INSPIRED HEARTS PUBLISHING

Inspired Hearts Publishing is an independently owned publishing house focused on multi-author, solo, and corporate book publications. Providing a platform for business owners to leverage their personal story, experience and expertise to grow their audience, and establish themselves as an expert in their industry.

Inspired Hearts Publishing elevates the stories of men and women who've overcame great hardships, experienced untraditional success and have been willing to carve their own path in life—stories of hope, inspiration, strength, resilience, love and transformation.

Learn more about Inspired Hearts Publishing: www.inspiredheartspublishing.com

INSPIRED HEARTS PUBLISHING

Inspired Hearts Publishing

Made in the USA
Monee, IL
07 January 2022

88312967R00089